The Corporate Strategy Matrix

THE CORPORATE STRATEGY MATRIX

Thomas H. Naylor

Basic Books, Inc., Publishers

NEW YORK

Library of Congress Cataloging-in-Publication Data

Naylor, Thomas H., 1936–
  The corporate strategy matrix.

  References: p. 276.
  Includes index.
  1. Corporate planning. 2. Strategic planning.
I. Title.
HD30.28.N393 1986   658.4'012   84–45316
ISBN 0–465–01425–9

Contents

Preface

WHILE WORKING as an outside consultant to the Shell Oil Company in 1978, I was first introduced to the idea that very often strategic planning involves the delicate balancing of two or more distinctly different economic forces. In the case of Shell, these forces consisted of a set of core business activities—which included gasoline, heating oil, agricultural chemicals, and the like—as well as a set of critical resources such as crude oil, refinery capacity, and engineering skills. Balancing the profitability requirements of individual businesses against limited supplies of critical resources becomes particularly difficult if, as was the case at Shell, the businesses share a number of common resources. To solve its business-resource balancing problem, Shell approached strategic planning as a team effort that brought together both business managers and resource managers. Although I was certainly impressed with the financial success Shell had achieved with its two-dimensional approach to strategic planning, at that time the uniqueness of the approach completely eluded me.

Roughly three years later I heard William Howard Beasley, III, then president of Velsicol Chemical Corporation, describe how his company had managed a dramatic recovery from a sea of burdensome environmental and legal problems. To achieve this turnabout, Velsicol put in place a team of strategy managers to coordinate a series of strategic activities that cut across all of the company's major functional areas, including finance, marketing, and production, as well as research and development. Basically, Velsicol's approach to strategic planning involved a cooperative effort between its strategy managers and its functional managers. That is, through a dual planning system, the company's strategic needs were balanced against its resource requirements. The rationale underlying Velsicol's two-dimensional approach to strategic planning was amazingly similar to the rationale upon which Shell's business-resource planning system was based. That is, the approach represented an attempt to address the fact that the company's business strategies required the use of a set of common interdependent resources.

A few months later, in May of 1982 to be exact, I heard Frederick O. Smith, founder and CEO of Federal Express, describe the way his company had dealt with such major new projects as ZAP-Mail, and with expansion into Canada and Europe. It suddenly occurred to me that Shell Oil, Velsicol Chemical, and Federal Express were all using a unique, two-dimensional approach to strategic planning that was to be found in very few other American companies. Furthermore, this approach to strategic planning seemed capable of eliminating some of the practical problems companies typically encountered when they attempted to confront interdependent business activities, this being especially troublesome in traditional hierarchical organizations.

At that point, I began to search for other American companies that might be employing a similar approach to strategic planning. Thus far, I have identified fourteen firms within the United States that use an approach to strategic planning based on two or more dimensions. While I make no claim to having done an exhaustive search of all major American corporations, I do believe that I have been able to identify most of the important examples of those companies that use what I call the *strategy matrix* to formulate and implement their long-term strategic plans.

In the fall of 1982, I introduced South Carolina Electric and Gas Company to the strategy matrix and a year later was directly involved in the implementation of the strategy matrix at Florida Power Corporation. In the spring of 1984, seven individuals who were responsible for implementing the strategy matrix in their respective companies were invited to participate in a seminar at the Fuqua School of Business at Duke University for the purpose of sharing their common experiences with the strategy matrix. This seminar, sponsored by the Center for Corporate Economics and Strategy at Duke University, included representatives from Florida Power, General Motors,

IBM, Shell Oil, South Carolina Electric and Gas, Squibb, and Velsicol Chemical. It was the first time, it seems, that these people had ever had any significant interaction with someone from another company who was involved in the implementation of the strategy matrix. As the seven representatives began to interact, it became increasingly apparent to me that each of them was using a very similar approach to strategic planning and that all were doing so for exactly the same kinds of reasons.

This book represents an attempt to summarize and systematize the experiences the aforementioned companies have had with the strategy matrix. The experiences of seven other companies that use this unique approach to strategic planning will also be examined. Those companies are Alcoa, Citibank, Dow Chemical, Dow-Corning, Federal Express, Intel, and Westinghouse Electric. I begin by defining the strategy matrix and spelling out the rationale underlying its use in organizations that are characterized by a high degree of business interdependence. After reviewing some of the important elements of strategic planning and matrix management, I proceed to consider four important applications of the strategy matrix: (1) portfolio analysis, which asks the question: Which businesses should we be in? (2) resource allocation: What level of commitment should we make to each business? (3) business strategy: How should each business compete? (4) international management: How should we compete in each country? In each case, I will define the specific strategic planning problem and indicate the limitations of traditional approaches to the solution of that problem. I then show how the strategy matrix has been used by specific companies to circumvent some of the problems associated with interdependent business activities. The entire book is based on the actual experiences of the fourteen companies I know to be using the strategy matrix. The book concludes with an examination of some of the managerial implications of the strategy matrix.

Many people have generously shared their experiences with the strategy matrix so that this book might become a reality. However, one person deserves special mention, for without his knowledge and experience with the strategy matrix, this book never would have been possible. William W. Reynolds, Economics Consultant at the Shell Oil Company, who introduced the strategy matrix there in 1972, was my guru, constructive critic, and source of considerable information about matrix management and team building. I shall always be indebted to him. Several other senior corporate executives made substantial contributions to the contents of this book and also deserve mention: David Barrington, Director of Strategic Planning, Velsicol Chemical Corporation; Dr. William Howard Beasley, III, Chairman and CEO, Lone Star Steel Company; Richard A. Druckman, Vice-President of Strategic Planning and M.I.S., Squibb Pharmaceutical Products Group; Martin Gerra, Manager of International Economics, IBM Corporation; Roger Gohrband, Director of Corporate Planning and Business Development, Dow Chemical Company; Robert D. Hazel, Vice-President of Communications and Planning, South Carolina Electric and Gas Company; William H. Hoffmann, Manager of Organization Planning, Aluminum Company of America; Abraham Katz, Director of Planning Systems, IBM Corporation; Patricia M. Marcotsis, Vice-President of Governmental and Regulatory Affairs, South Carolina Electric and Gas Company; John C. Marous, President of Industries and International Group, Westinghouse Electric Corporation; George C. Moore, Vice-President of Engineering Services, Florida Power Corporation; Michael E. Naylor, General Director of Corporate Strategic Planning, General Motors Corporation; Lee H. Scott, President, Florida Power Corporation; Frederick O. Smith, CEO, Federal Express Corporation; Robert S. Springmier, Controller, Dow-Corning Corporation; Virgil O. Summer, Chairman and CEO, SCANA Corporation; Professor William Alberts, University of Washington. And finally, substantial editorial assistance through several revisions of this manuscript was provided by Yvonne M. Lamvik, always with a high degree of professionalism and good cheer.

The Corporate Strategy Matrix

1

THE CASE FOR THE
STRATEGY MATRIX

WHEN General Motors announced on January 10, 1984, that it was reorganizing its five automobile manufacturing divisions into large- and small-car groups, there was no mention in the business press that GM was, in fact, emulating a style of planning management successfully used for over a decade by such companies as IBM, Shell Oil, Dow Chemical, and Federal Express. This style of management is known as the *strategy matrix*. Under the reorganization, GM will continue to market automobiles through the same five divisions it has been operating since 1916—Buick, Cadillac, Chevrolet, Oldsmobile, and Pontiac. Product development, design, and engineering, however, will be consolidated under the purview of two newly created, self-contained business units. Small cars will be developed and manufactured by the Chevrolet-Pontiac-GM Canada Group, with intermediate- and large-sized cars engineered and produced by the Buick-Cadillac-Oldsmobile Group. While the five auto divisions continue to exist, they have, in essence, become primarily marketing arms of the two new groups.

GM's decision to implement the strategy matrix was based on the increasing difficulty traditional divisionalized companies have in planning, organizing, and controlling businesses, critical resources, strategies, and international operations that are all characterized by a high degree of market interdependence and shared resources. But such characteristics are precisely why more than one dozen major American companies turned to the strategy matrix in the 1970s.[1]

A Case Study

The strategy matrix is a participatory planning management system that makes extensive use of management teams to overcome some of the frustrations traditional hierarchical organizations experience in coping with interdependent business activities. Some insight can be gained into the concepts underlying the strategy matrix, as well as some of the reasons that a number of companies have adopted it, by considering the case of Dow-Corning, the company that first introduced the strategy matrix in 1968. A wholly owned joint venture of Dow Chemical Company and Corning Glass, Dow-Corning produces and markets a class of synthetic material known as silicones. The evolution of Dow-Corning's organization structure —from a highly centralized functional organization to a decentralized divisional organization and finally to a matrix-like organization—will serve to illustrate some of the important features of the strategy matrix. This example should also illustrate some of the limitations of traditional hierarchical organizations and suggest ways in which the strategy matrix can be used to overcome these limitations.

FUNCTIONAL ORGANIZATION

From its inception in 1943 until 1962, Dow-Corning was operated as a traditional, highly centralized functional organization. That is, the usual corporate functions of finance, marketing, manufacturing, and research and development were thoroughly centralized even though the company operated on a worldwide basis. Such an organization structure is, indeed, typical of most new organizations. In a functional organization, planning, budgeting, and implementation are all activities pursued along strictly functional lines. With a small, single-product business, such an organization structure represents a relatively straightforward way in which to organize the activities of the firm. In the single-product business, functional managers not only formulate plans and budgets but are also responsible for the implementation of these plans. Planning and budgeting are both essentially single-dimensional activities in a functional organization.

Suppose, however—as was the case at Dow-Corning—that as the firm begins to grow, additional products are introduced. In the single-product firm, all of the company's functional resources are channeled into a single product. In the multiproduct firm, on the other hand, functional resources must be shared. For example, in a functional organization, the marketing manager is responsible for the marketing activities of all of the products in the product line. The production manager is directly responsible for the manufacturing process of the goods the company makes. Likewise, the manager of human resource development must provide people with the appropriate skills and backgrounds to support all of the products.

Suppose that a CEO of a multiproduct functionally organized firm observes that a particular product appears to be performing quite poorly. Sales are down, costs are up, and profits are plummeting. Upon inquiring of the marketing manager as to the nature of the problem, the marketing manager suggests that the problem lies in the quality of the product and the relatively high cost of producing it. "We are doing all we can to promote this product, but it is very difficult to sell such a poor quality, expensive product." The production manager, on the other hand, feels that the product is basically very good and that production costs are within reason. For him the problem is primarily one of marketing, and he feels that the marketing manager is simply not pushing the product in the marketplace. Finally, there is the chief financial officer who feels that both the marketing manager and the production manager are to blame. He argues that the production operations are highly inefficient and that the marketing manager is spending entirely too much on advertising without any regard for the benefits from specific media forms. In other words, neither the marketing manager, the production manager, nor the chief financial officer is willing to assume overall responsibility for the profitability of the particular product. Therein lies the problem of attempting to manage a multiproduct firm with a highly centralized, functional organization.

The introduction of additional products imposes a second dimension on the firm's management system, namely, a product dimension. As Dow-Corning discovered, with each addition to its product line, increased stress was placed on its single-dimension functional organization. With the company selling products to virtually every industry in the United States, as well as to industrially developed nations throughout the world, coordination of the interdependent financial, marketing, and production activities became increasingly difficult as the company's product lines continued to expand. What the company eventually learned is that product planning tends to get severely shortchanged in a functional organization.

DIVISIONAL ORGANIZATION

In response to the stress imposed on its simple functional organization by market diversification and rapid growth, Dow-Corning in 1962 restructured its original functional organization into a divisional organization similar to the one illustrated in figure 1-1. The company was divided into five product-oriented profit centers or divisions, each having its own manufacturing, marketing, product development, and accounting functions, thus reflecting the two-dimensional nature of the company's business activities—products and functions. The divisional structure that evolved at Dow-Corning resembled the one employed by General Motors for over fifty years when it had its separate Chevrolet, Oldsmobile, Pontiac, and Cadillac divisions. Although functional coordination within product divisions improved under Dow-Corning's reorganization, harmony between product divisions, as well as between the divisions and corporate staff, actually worsened. To understand why these problems persisted within the reorganized structure, we must examine the interdependent nature of some of the company's product lines. Dow-Corning's products shared many common resources, such as marketing, technology, and research and development. In addition, some products were sold in highly interdependent markets, which created joint demand functions. Unfortunately, the divisional organization structure failed to encourage the cooperation and coordination necessary among divisions to improve overall efficiency and effectiveness. Business plans were formulated and implemented as though each business existed in a vacuum.

Even after Dow-Corning's single-dimension functional structure was replaced by a divisional structure encompassing two dimensions, planning, budgeting, and implementation were still being carried out as

8

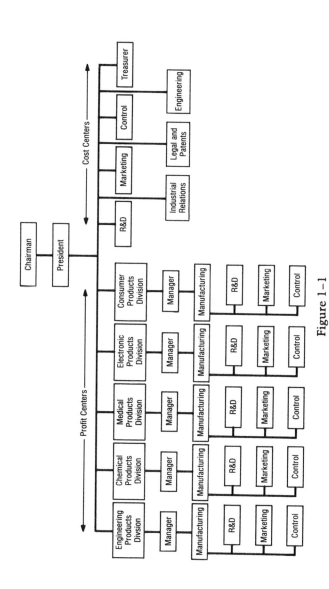

Figure 1–1

The Dow-Corning Divisionalized Organization

SOURCE: Robert S. Springmier, Dow-Corning Corporation

before. The difference now being that the product dimension was the focus of attention rather than the functional dimension. Each product division was still managed in isolation, oblivious, as it were, to the interdependence of the products. The divisions were almost islands unto themselves, particularly with regard to shared resources. All that really had happened at Dow-Corning was that one single-dimensional management system replaced another. And so, the inefficiencies caused by insufficient coordination of the functional resources persisted despite a change in organization structure.

What was painfully obvious was that neither Dow-Corning's initial functional organization structure nor its later divisional structure had really come to grips with the company's two-dimensional management problems. Not until six years later did the company finally generate a management system capable of dealing simultaneously with the functional and product dimensions of its business activities.

STRATEGY MATRIX

When Dow-Corning's new CEO, William C. Coggin, introduced the strategy matrix in 1968, his goal was to resolve two very specific problems: (1) the multidimensional nature of the company's planning, budgeting, and implementation activities and (2) the extreme interdependence of the company's product divisions. The initial version of the strategy matrix adopted by Dow-Corning appears in figure 1–2. As we have previously noted, in the company's original

10

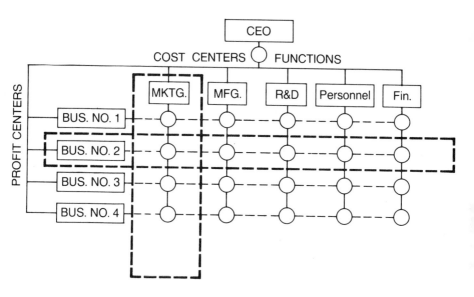

Figure 1-2

The Dow-Corning Strategy Matrix

SOURCE: Robert S. Springmier, Dow-Corning Corporation

functional organization structure, planning, budgeting, and implementation were the responsibilities of functional managers since no product managers existed. Upon introduction of the divisionalized structure, these management functions were reassigned exclusively to the product division managers. But then, with the introduction of the strategy matrix (figure 1-2), planning and budgeting became joint responsibilities between business managers and functional managers. Implementation activities remained exclusively the responsibility of functional managers.

While the businesses are roughly analogous to the original product divisions, they no longer operate as stand-alone divisions. Rather, they compete for a pool of shared resources over which they have no direct control. The functional managers control the company's scarce resources.

Each business within Dow-Corning is organized as a profit center, with its own full-time manager responsible for short-term profitability and long-term performance. The business managers assess the external opportunities and internal capabilities for their own product line, develop five-year objectives and strategies that are consistent with these opportunities and capabilities, and propose specific operating plans and budgets for implementing strategies.

The functions are also organized as corporatewide cost centers, each possessing a full-time manager responsible for "professionalism" and the efficient allocation of the company's resources across the portfolio of businesses. These functional managers review the plans and budgets developed by the businesses, an especially necessary task when critical resource constraints place limitations on the business plans. Ultimately, the functional managers determine how all of the business plans will be implemented since it is they who control the company's resources. Business managers and resource managers at Dow-Corning are both at the same managerial rank.

To accommodate the businesses, the functional resources are organized as illustrated in figure 1–2. For example, marketing is subdivided such that a specific manager is assigned marketing responsibility for a particular business. These managers have dual reporting channels. They report both to the overall marketing director and to the manager of one of the businesses. Each of the other functions is organized in a similar fashion. Through this dual reporting system, Dow-Corning has achieved interfunctional balance and harmony regarding profit and growth targets. And it has not had to sacrifice functional efficiency and integrity in order to achieve this degree of coordination.

The planning process at Dow-Corning encompasses three major activities: formulation of objectives, planning, and budgeting. First, each business establishes five-year objectives and goals, as well as specific one-year targets. The resources necessary to meet these objectives and goals are then allocated by the functional managers to the business plans. At the third level of activity, these plans are translated into detailed cost-center budgets for the coming year. The results of each of these activities are reviewed carefully by Dow-Corning's executive committee at each stage of the planning process. The principal benefit of such a review is the reconciliation of the business and functional dimensions of Dow-Corning's strategy matrix.

Fundamentally, what differentiates the strategy matrix from other planning and management systems is that planning and budgeting activities are seen as shared responsibilities that involve both business managers and functional managers. The key element, of course, is the manner in which planning is executed within a given structure. This, we believe, is even more important than the type of organization structure actually employed by the enterprise. The fact that Dow-Corning happens to have a matrix-type organization structure is incidental to the applicability of the strategy matrix, which can be applied to any type of organization structure—functional, divisional, or matrix. In each case, planning involves a cooperative effort between at least two sets of managers. At Dow-Corning this has meant cooperation between business managers and functional managers. In the case of Federal Express, another firm that uses the strategy matrix, the relevant managers are strategy managers and functional managers. And, at the Dow Chemical Company, the strategy matrix involves the sharing of planning responsibilities among three tiers—country managers, functional managers, and product managers. We must point out, however, that in all three companies, the actual implementation of plans is the primary responsibility of the functional managers who control the organization's critical resources.

As we have seen, the strategy matrix creates a participatory planning and management system that facilitates the involvement of both business managers and functional managers in the formulation and implementation of a company's plans. Furthermore, the matrix encourages a style of management that is characterized by cooperation, trust, and team building among managers. Decision making is pushed deeper into the organization, and more people are thus allowed to participate in the decision-making process than is usually the case in the typical hierarchical organization. It also attempts to restore some degree of small-company flexibility to large, complex organizations.

Since Dow-Corning first began using the strategy matrix in 1968, it has been introduced by a number of other major companies. IBM and Shell Oil have employed it since 1972, Citibank and Federal Express since 1974, and Velsicol Chemical and Westinghouse International since 1979. Squibb introduced it in 1981, South Carolina Electric and Gas in 1982, and Florida Power came on board in 1983. Alcoa, Dow Chemical, and Northwest Industries are a few of the other major corporations using the strategy matrix.

Rationale for the Strategy Matrix

The appeal of the strategy matrix is based in no small part upon its ability to overcome some of the major deficiencies of divisional and functional organizations. While most large companies today are divisionalized into operating companies or businesses of one sort or another, the individual business units are typically organized along functional lines, including, among many other possibilities, finance, marketing, production, personnel, and engineering. Four somewhat interrelated problems with divisional and functional organizations provide the rationale underlying the use of the strategy matrix.

15

BUSINESS INTERDEPENDENCE

The typical manufacturing company in the United States consists of a collection or portfolio of businesses, such as GM's, which consists of Buicks, Cadillacs, Chevrolets, Oldsmobiles, and Pontiacs, as well as some other businesses. Strategic questions associated with the management of a portfolio of businesses are (1) Which businesses should the company be in? and (2) How should they be financed? Providing answers to questions of this nature prompted a new approach to strategic planning known as the *portfolio* approach, which evolved in the late 1960s.

The concept of portfolio planning originated with The Boston Consulting Group (BCG) and was popularized by them and by McKinsey and Company, who introduced the concept at General Electric and proceeded to divide the company into the well-known forty-three *strategic business units*. As defined by General Electric and others, a strategic business unit (SBU) is "a reasonably self-sufficient business that does not meet head-on with other businesses in making the major management decisions necessary." Such portfolio planning has been widely emulated by numerous management consulting firms. Indeed, by 1979, according to a recent survey by Phillippe Haspeslagh, 35 percent of the Fortune 1,000 companies and 55 percent of the Fortune 250 companies were using portfolio planning.[2]

In recent years, however, the whole concept of portfolio planning has come under careful scrutiny by many companies, including General Electric, Texas

Instruments, Xerox, and Mexico's Grupo Industrial Alpha. All of these firms had enthusiastically embraced the portfolio approach but have now encountered some well-publicized problems. General Electric's attempt to buy its way into the microprocessor business (after selling off its computer mainframe business ten years earlier) is one illustration of the use of a methodology that may have outlived its usefulness. Texas Instrument's recent financial losses, Xerox's notorious problems in coping with Japanese competition, and the Mexican government's $680 million bailout of Grupo Alpha (long before the devaluation of the peso) are other examples that illustrate some of the problems attributed to the portfolio approach as it is presently practiced. As we shall see, there are, in fact, some very serious practical problems associated with the strategic business unit concept of portfolio planning. Most of these problems stem from the fact that, in actual practice, strategic business units are often not independent of each other in the important areas of critical resources and market demand.

Before proceeding further, we should consider the whole question of what precisely constitutes an SBU. What are some of the possible consequences of improperly defining an SBU? Consider, for example, General Electric's decision, over ten years ago, to sell its computer mainframe business, a decision that was applauded in many quarters at the time as a sound application of modern portfolio theory. The company, so it was perceived, had wisely shed itself of what The Boston Consulting Group calls a "dog."

Ten years later, however, General Electric's decision to divest itself of its computer business presents itself in a quite different light. In reality, what the company had done was sell off the very technology that might have enabled it to enter the microprocessor business much sooner than it eventually did. Thus, General Electric has recently found itself forced to play economic catch-up. Because microprocessors are vital to many of its other businesses, it has had to buy—at premium prices—its way into the microprocessor business.

If we look back at General Electric's planning process in the early 1970s, we note the domination of this process by the managers of the SBUs. Since each SBU with General Electric was treated as a stand-alone business, insufficient attention was given to the possible implications for broader, corporatewide functional planning or critical resource planning. The strategy matrix, with its emphasis on the participation of both business and resource managers, attempts to reduce the risks involved in incorrectly defining—that is, isolating—an SBU and later having to pay the consequences.

A second practical problem is that the SBU approach implicitly assumes that it is possible to define businesses in such a way that they operate independently with regard to manufacturing and marketing. While it is possible to treat the operating companies owned by a diversified conglomerate such as Northwest Industries as independent, it is quite impossible to regard individual businesses within particular operating companies, such as General Battery or Velsicol Chemical, as independent businesses. In the real world, many businesses not only share the same manufacturing and production resources, they also generate products that are either substitutes or complements of each other and have, therefore, interdependent markets. This is particularly true of process-oriented industries such as petroleum, chemicals, electric utilities, and steel.

And it is here that we arrive at the heart of the matter and see why General Motors turned to the matrix in its recently announced reorganization. Since one line of automobile is a direct substitute for every other type of automobile produced by GM, it follows that demand for the company's five lines is completely interdependent. But if this is so, does it make sense to operate separate design, separate development, and separate engineering departments for each of the five auto businesses? With its reorganization, GM answered "no," and so these functions were consolidated into each of the two groups. But then another question arises. If the large-car group shares common product development resources, doesn't it make sense to share manufacturing resources as well? In essence, what GM did by announcing the reorganization was acknowledge the complete interdependence of product development, manufacturing, and marketing of its five auto businesses. The matrix should give GM the flexibility to fine-tune its large-car, small-car mix in response to changes in competition and the price of gasoline.

In light of the above discussion, Xerox's decision to apply the SBU approach to its portfolio of copiers appears to be particularly ill conceived. With each line of copiers competing with every other line of copiers in the marketplace, as well as competing for manufacturing resources, the choice of an SBU approach does not appear to make much sense. In chapter 3 I will demonstrate that the analytical tools of The Boston Consulting Group and the other portfolio planning consulting firms are, quite simply, inadequate to approach problems of this type. Without hesitation, I believe that it will take something more creative than conventional portfolio planning to protect Xerox from Japanese competition.

The portfolio approach to strategic planning assumes, among other things, that in the case of a large decentralized company, the only resource the parent company allocates to each SBU is cash. This assumption raises a third practical problem related to the SBU concept. For instance, once the parent company has approved an individual SBU's strategic plan and budget, corporate management is assumed to play little or no role in how a particular SBU allocates its resources. I can think of countless examples, however, where the parent corporation not only controls the allocation of investment dollars but the allocation of one or more other critical resources as well. This is the case with the petroleum and petrochemical industries, as well as with electric utilities, pulp and paper, and most kinds of mining.

Yet another problem with the portfolio approach arises when companies attempt to force a fictitious independence on their SBUs. In doing so, a corporation may fail to take advantage of certain synergies and economies of scale offered by its portfolio of businesses. Again, General Motors serves as an excellent illustration of this problem. Implicit in the company's reorganization is the recognition that in the past it had not taken full advantage of some of the possible economies of scale in product development and manufacturing. This same problem, compounded by an excessive increase in the number of businesses in its portfolio, triggered the financial difficulties experienced recently by Grupo Alpha in Mexico.

While one of the principal reasons for the increasing appeal of the strategy matrix is that it overcomes many of the limitations of the portfolio approach in coping with the problem of interdependent SBUs, there are other forms of interdependence not directly related to the portfolio problem that can be addressed by the matrix. For example, at Velsicol Chemical, Federal Express, South Carolina Electric and Gas, and Florida Power, it was interdependent business strategies that provided the rationale for the use of the strategy matrix. On another front, Alcoa, Citibank, and Westinghouse International were drawn to the matrix because of the interdependence of their complex and widely scattered international businesses. In his bestseller, *Megatrends*, John Naisbitt forecasts the creation of a globally interdependent society that will be characterized by increased information-processing requirements, government and business decentralization, participatory management, networking, more focus on long-term issues and goals, and multiple-option decision making.[3] Without exception, these are precisely the kinds of forces that are now motivating corporate executives to seriously consider adoption of the strategy matrix.

ZERO-SUM MANAGEMENT

A particularly troublesome consequence of typical divisional/functional organization structures is the pervasiveness of the zero-sum management style that characterizes so many hierarchically organized firms. In game theory, where the term originated, a zero-sum game results in a situation where one player's gain exactly equals the loss of the other player. Such zero-sum thinking is widespread in most major American companies. And by no means is it limited to the most obvious area of conflict—namely, labor-management relations. Thanks to the influence of Japanese, German, and Scandinavian management practices, such formerly volatile issues as labor-management relations have been defused as a more cooperative approach is replacing the zero-sum mentality. Such concepts as quality circles and union representation on boards of directors are but two examples of this trend. The idea that labor is an important partner in the success of the firm has increasing appeal to enlightened corporate executives, and examples of increased cooperation between labor and management abound. I can cite the changes General Motors introduced at Lordstown, Ohio, the Japanese management of the Kawasaki plant in Nebraska, and the appearance of employee-owned companies, such as Chicago Northwestern Railroad, United Parcel Service, Vermont Asbestos, and South Bend Lathe.[4]

But the zero-sum management style still pervades

other important areas of management. For example, we see it in large decentralized companies in the relationship between corporate management and the management of the individual operating companies or business units owned by the parent company. The conflicts in these cases revolve around such issues as strategic planning, resource allocation, budgeting, and control. For instance, who controls the strategic plan of an operating company is an issue ripe with potential for conflict. Typically, the general manager of an operating company negotiates with corporate management for investment resources, such resources being based upon a set of goals, objectives, and strategies proposed by the operating company itself. The individual operating company, or strategic business unit, attempts to obtain as large an investment as possible from the parent company for as little cost as possible in terms of expected return to the corporation.

Corporate management, on the other hand, wants to minimize its investment in operating companies and seeks a high return from each of its business units. Fierce conflicts are not uncommon between corporate management and operating company managers, and a type of "we" versus "them" syndrome sometimes arises over the control of the division-planning process. Indeed, in some companies, there is almost open warfare between division management and corporate management. At IBM, Shell Oil, and Squibb—companies that in the past experienced divisive zero-sum management syndromes—the strategy matrix has been introduced and used as a corporate resource allocation tool, which has helped reduce the magnitude of the conflicts of the type just discussed.

Another form of divisiveness encouraged by many decentralized companies is competition among operating companies for markets. In some companies, the alleged efficiencies associated with decentralized management may be negated by back-stabbing, cut-throat competition among operating company managers. Avoiding such conflicts provided part of the motivation for General Motors and Dow-Corning to adopt the matrix.

Zero-sum attitudes also constitute a big problem for functional management. As previously indicated, most firms are, ultimately, organized around a number of specific functional activities such as finance, accounting, manufacturing, sales, and marketing. Even in the case of highly decentralized conglomerates, individual operating companies are typically organized along functional lines. And this is true for both single-product and multiproduct operating companies. In some cases, functional managers provide resources in support of a single product, in others they support a portfolio of products. No matter how you slice it, functional managers play an extremely important role in most American companies. It is they who control the scarce resources necessary to produce the goods and services provided by the firm.

In all too many companies, however, functional managers lord over jealously guarded fiefdoms. They manage their functional activities as though they were running an independent business rather than providing one of several critical resources necessary for the survival and profitability of the company as a whole. Indeed, overly zealous corporate executives frequently encourage their functional managers in this feudal behavior. Executives who hold a distorted view of the applicability of the nineteenth-century competitive model to intracompany activities are the source of many a company's problems. For example, an industry in which this form of zero-sum conflict tends to be particularly extreme is the electric utility industry. Executives in electric utilities often manipulate their functional resources as if they were political territories rather than interdependent activities, the smooth operation of which requires a high degree of cooperation among functional managers.

The present crisis regarding nuclear power plants provides a good example of this kind of zero-sum conflict in the electric utility industry. In the 1960s and early 1970s, when most nuclear power plants were being designed, nuclear engineers were the high priests of the industry—omnipotent beings who could do no wrong. Consider the case of the Tennessee Valley Authority (TVA), which made the largest commitment to nuclear power of any utility in the country. The board of directors of the TVA originally backed the construction of a total of seventeen nuclear reactors. By 1982, however, eight of these had been either deferred or canceled. In 1985, the TVA ordered that its $1 billion nuclear power plant at Browns Ferry, Alabama, remain inactive indefinitely until it can be operated safely. This shutdown was ordered because the plant had been plagued with

25

problems ever since a fire broke out in the plant in 1975. A TVA worker, who was using a lighted candle to check equipment for air leaks, had accidentally caused the fire. The decision to invest so heavily in nuclear power had been made by a small group of very influential nuclear engineers and was then rubber-stamped all the way up to the board of directors, where the decision was again approved. The members of this board of directors were former politicians who knew nothing about nuclear technology. In other words, critical decisions were being made within a single department of an enterprise without benefit of consultation with other functional managers. The result, of course, is that TVA customers have paid a very high price in increased rates for the self-serving decisions made by a group of technicians who were operating in a vacuum.

In January of 1984, a week-long chain of disasters put the nuclear power industry through its darkest days since the Three Mile Island accident. According to the *New York Times*, within a few days of each other, Commonwealth Edison was denied a license by the Nuclear Regulatory Commission to operate its $3.4 billion twin-reactor Bryon plant, the Public Service Company of Indiana canceled work on its $2.5 billion Marble Hill nuclear plant, and Cincinnati Gas and Electric announced that it would convert its $1.6 billion William H. Zimmer nuclear facility, which was 99 percent complete, into a coal-fired plant.[5] By midyear 1984, four electric utilities in the United States were facing possible bankruptcy. It should be obvious from this depressing list that if ever there was an industry in need of a radical change in its management style, it is the electric power industry. To reduce the risk of replicating these costly errors, South Carolina Electric and Gas, as well as Florida Power, has implemented use of the strategy matrix. Particular emphasis in these two utilities is being placed on business strategies managed by strategy teams. By cutting across multiple functional lines, these teams provide corporate management with a much clearer, reality-based view of the company as a whole.

One of the principal aims, then, of the strategy matrix is to confront the myopic, zero-sum management style that is characteristic of so many American companies. Indeed, this may very well be the single most important contribution of the matrix.

ALIENATION

A third problem contributing to recent interest in the strategy matrix is not unrelated to the problem of interdependence and zero-sum management. Corporate executives all across the country are increasingly concerned with the problem of alienation. Hardly a month goes by in which there is not at least one article in the business press about some well-known corporate executive who has opted out of corporate life in order to pursue a quieter, more reflective existence far removed from the management of a major corporation. Often referred to as a midlife identity crisis, this phenomenon may well be caused by the absence of a sense of purpose or meaning in the lives of many of these high-level executives. In all too many firms, senior executives are forced to subscribe to the values of the company in order to advance up the corporate ladder. The values they must embrace often place too much emphasis on greed, the acquisition of power, and the desire to dominate and manipulate others. For such executives, motivation comes not from internal personal goals but from recognition and approval by others. Eventually, this type of behavior results in anxiety, depression, feelings of emptiness, and burnout. Some executives turn to drugs and alcohol to combat the loneliness and emptiness caused by their complete alienation from the corporate environment. Indeed, it is not surprising to learn that there are over three hundred stress-management programs in existence in the United States today.

Although it has not traditionally been the responsibility of corporations to provide purpose to the lives of their managers and employees, the costs associated with a lack of meaning can be enormous, and can show up in the form of absenteeism, high turnover, low morale, decreased productivity, and reduced profitability. With its emphasis on participatory management and team building, the strategy matrix represents an alternative to traditional divisional and functional organization structures. The matrix provides an environment that is conducive to personal growth and the search for meaning.

Additional evidence of the problem of managerial alienation can be found by looking at the growing number of frustrated executives who have exchanged the security of the large corporation for the high risk of starting their own businesses. Furthermore, we are observing that recent M.B.A. graduates are increasingly seeking employment in smaller firms, especially those that are perceived to encourage entrepreneurship. Some large companies—IBM, Control Data, Hewlett-Packard, and Minnesota Mining and Manufacturing, to name but a few—are fighting back by co-opting the techniques of the new entrepreneurs. The term *intrapreneurialism* has been coined to describe attempts by large corporations to replicate an entrepreneurial atmosphere in a large bureaucracy. IBM's personal computer, for example, was developed by a group of employees who were freed from corporate red tape and given the resources to create what has become a highly successful new product.

As we shall see, one of the principal advantages of the strategy matrix is that it helps generate a small-business atmosphere in large organizations. It provides an atmosphere in which more people can have a piece of the action and a feeling that what they do actually matters. Experience indicates that with the strategy matrix, not only is more human energy generated by corporate managers, but there also exists a greater possibility of developing what economics consultant William W. Reynolds of Shell Oil calls *breakaway strategies*—those seminal, innovative ideas that potentially could provide a company with the opportunity to make quantum leaps ahead of competitors. The Super Hub of Federal Express in Memphis, Tennessee, and the IBM personal computer are examples of breakaway strategies.

INFLEXIBILITY

Business interdependence, zero-sum management style, and alienating management practices all lead to corporate inflexibility, a concept we define as an inability to respond rapidly to an ever-changing environment. The very lack of flexibility in divisional/functional organizations is a key fourth reason that the strategy matrix is gaining in its appeal to senior corporate executives. Referring to Shell Oil's experience with the strategy matrix, William W. Reynolds has said, "The key to Shell's success with the strategy matrix is the flexibility it provides in responding to a dynamic external environment characterized by the on-again, off-again availability of crude oil in world markets, erratic oil prices, and declining consumer demand."

We shall briefly outline some of the forces that have contributed to the need for greater corporate flexibility in responding to changes in the external environment. Continuously since the 1930s, federal, state, and local governments have all increased their regulatory activities. This pattern persisted until the late 1970s, when the Carter administration began to reverse the trend. The Reagan administration has followed suit by dramatically reducing the level of federal regulation. Government regulation played an important role in inducing IBM, Velsicol Chemical, and Squibb to implement the strategy matrix.

At the end of the Johnson administration, when the U.S. Justice Department filed an antitrust suit against IBM, severe constraints were placed on the company's ability to maneuver in a rapidly changing, high-technology field. With the introduction of the matrix in 1972, however, IBM was able to achieve a degree of flexibility that might not otherwise have been possible, given the veil of the Justice Department's lawsuit. The company continued to grow and to prosper during the 1970s, despite the government's threat of litigation. Similarly, Velsicol Chemical's use of the matrix was directly attributable to a barrage of legal actions taken against it in the mid-1970s due to its marketing of a number of extremely toxic chemicals. And, as with many other pharmaceutical companies, Squibb has had to cope with the FDA's very tight regulations for the marketing of new drugs. Again, a need for increased flexibility in a difficult regulatory environment contributed to Squibb's interest in the matrix. In yet another industry, uncertainty about the likelihood of suitable rate relief from state public service commissions, as well as the stringent policies of the Nuclear Regulatory Commission, contributed to South Carolina Electric and Gas's and Florida Power's interest in the strategy matrix.

Added domestic and foreign competition and rapid product obsolescence have been the motivating forces behind some companies deciding to adopt the strategy matrix. Competitive forces and technological change were definitely among the factors contributing to the adoption of the matrix by IBM, Federal Express, and Dow Chemical. The increased complexity associated with a dynamic international environment brought Alcoa, Citibank, and Westinghouse to the strategy matrix, and expanding sensitivity to the needs of both their customers and their employees influenced the decision of Florida Power and South Carolina Electric and Gas to adopt it.

Finally, what Alvin Toffler[6] has called the "demassification of society" has also set loose forces demanding increased flexibility on the part of large and small organizations. That "big" is no longer necessarily beautiful is a dawning realization and has already led in some corporations to the demassification of such functions as production, distribution, and communications. Examples of demassification include the breakup of AT&T, the microcomputer revolution, and some of the new technologies that may diminish our need to build any more large-scale electric power plants. Such forces as these will all generate pressures within organizations for an increase in flexibility. Once again we see how well the strategy matrix stacks up as a viable alternative when companies are faced with the need to respond rapidly to environmental transformations.

Important Prerequisites

Although the strategy matrix is characterized by maximum flexibility and adapts well to a wide variety of organization structures and management styles, there are three elements that are absolutely critical to the actual implementation of this approach to management. First, senior management must appreciate the advantages of cooperation, trust, and team build-ing over the values typically associated with tradi-tional organizations, whether these were hierarchical or pyramid structured. Management personnel must also be receptive to what *Megatrends* author John Naisbitt calls "networking." In his book, Naisbitt says that "The failure of hierarchies to solve society's problems forced people to talk to one another—that was the beginning of 'networks.' "[7] As I hope has been obvious throughout the discussions in this chapter, the very essence of the strategy matrix is grounded in the concept of networking. It provides the rationale and a logical structure on which the strategy matrix stands. Some companies may already possess participatory styles of management condu-cive to networking, but for others it may be a very long, slow process. The matrix is not a rigid, mecha-nistic technique that has been mastered by the newest breed of M.B.A.s. Rather, it is a highly flexible, intu-itive style of management. In addition, it should not be approached as though it were the latest executive toy, for example, as if it were a personal computer. As we shall see in the next chapter, the strategy matrix is an incredibly subtle and sophisticated concept, one that should be approached with caution and subtlety in return.

The second requirement for successful implemen-tation of the matrix is that the firm's senior manage-ment must also be committed to formal strategic planning. They must be willing to give in-depth con-sideration to such questions as (1) Which businesses should the company be in? (2) How should they be financed? (3) What level of investment should be made in each business? (4) How should the businesses compete in the marketplace? (5) In which geographic locations should the company be doing business? The answers to these questions are called *strategies.*

But goals and objectives, strategies and corporate policies are, in the final analysis, determined by the personal values, ethical principles, and sense of purpose of senior management. Since the strategy matrix rests so heavily on mutual trust and cooperation, as well as informal communication, it must be linked to a planning process based on a corporate culture and management philosophy that is compatible with these.

Therefore, the third prerequisite to implementing the strategy matrix is that the company must have a corporate culture that is consistent with participatory management and team building. Without too much stretch of the imagination, we can assume that the management of General Motors must be experiencing a high degree of culture shock with the implementation of a reorganized structure. At least on the surface, the matrix would appear to be antithetical to GM's corporate culture. The fact that Velsicol Chemical, Florida Power, and South Carolina Electric and Gas were all in the hands of new CEOs probably has made it easier for them to overcome some of the cultural resistance to the matrix.

Matrix Management: Fact and Fiction

To recapitulate, the strategy matrix is a participatory planning management system in which planning takes place along two or more dimensions, such as businesses and functions, while the implementation of plans always follows functional lines. Thus, a matrix approach to the formulation, evaluation, and coordination of business plans is combined with a functional approach to the implementation of these plans. And, as we shall see in the next chapter, the strategy matrix is, in fact, a special case of a somewhat controversial style of management known as *matrix management*. The unique feature underlying matrix management is the disarmingly simple idea that a manager may have two or more bosses. At Dow-Corning, for example, this is illustrated by the marketing planning manager who reports to a particular business manager and to the marketing manager.

For over twenty years, strong empirical evidence of the successful use of matrix management has been accumulated from such organizations as IBM, Control Data, NASA, Northern Telecom, and Rockwell International. Yet, in spite of this evidence, matrix management has not escaped criticism. In their recent best-selling book, *In Search of Excellence*, Peters and Waterman claim that none of their so-called "excellent companies" are run by matrix management and that those who once used it have abandoned it.[8] Specifically, these authors had this to say about matrix management:

People aren't sure to whom they should report for what. The most critical problem, it seems, is that in the name of "balance," everything is somehow hooked to everything else. The organization gets paralyzed because the structure not only does not make priorities clear, *it automatically dilutes priorities.* In effect, it says to people down the line: "Everything is important: pay equal attention to everything." This message is paralyzing.[9]

. . . it virtually always ceases to be innovative, often after just a short while. It has particular difficulty in executing the basics (the authority structure is uniquely weak). It also regularly degenerates into anarchy and rapidly becomes bureaucratic and noncreative. The long-term direction of the matrixed organization is usually not clear.[10]

These are very strong statements. But are they true? In the first place, if one examines Peters and Waterman's list of sixty-two "excellent companies,"[11] one finds that during the 1979–1980 time period in which the study was being conducted, at least eleven of these firms were actually using matrix management,[12] and four—Dow Chemical, IBM, Intel, and Westinghouse—were using the strategy matrix as well. And, despite their obvious distaste for matrix management, the authors neglect to provide a single example of where it has failed.

It is one thing to suggest that an organization's structure should be kept lean and simple. It is quite another thing, however, to suggest ways in which an organization should integrate complex interdependencies. In their book, Peters and Waterman seem to be suggesting that matrix management is the cause of organizational complexity in interdependent organizations. Quite the contrary! The reality is that matrix management provides a structure capable of coping with the inherent complexity that already exists within the organization. In summary, Peters and Waterman's attacks on matrix management might have been more credible had they provided some supporting evidence to justify their claims.

Benefits

Contrary to the views expressed by Peters and Waterman, there are, indeed, a number of significant benefits associated with a matrix approach to planning management. The principal benefit of the strategy matrix is that its multidimensional approach to planning provides a unique mechanism for approaching interdependent businesses, resources, strategies, and international operations. Possible reductions or elimination of some of the inefficiencies associated with shared resources and market interdependence are advantages that immediately come to mind. The matrix can also provide a positive alternative to zero-sum management, which may then reduce alienation problems by encouraging cooperative, participatory management. Since the strategy matrix brings non-managers into the planning process, it often contributes to a stronger sense of meaning and increased productivity among employees other than just managers. Not only does the strategy matrix involve a higher degree of management participation than is usually the case within hierarchical organizations, but it also provides increased organizational flexibility combined with an ability to respond quickly to changes in the external environment. In turn, this enhanced ability to react can then, and often does, lead to improved market responsiveness and operational efficiencies based on more effective communication between business and functional managers. By virtue of the fact that the strategy matrix penetrates more deeply into the organization, it paves the way for the emergence of more profit-oriented managers throughout the organization.

In recent years, a number of articles have appeared in the popular business press that have been quite harsh on formal corporate planning. Many of these articles have criticized the alleged gap that exists between planning and implementation. Why this criticism persists is astonishing. The very nature of the strategy matrix is such that it helps close the gap between planning and implementation. Business and functional managers participate in the planning process. Business managers help coordinate the implementation of plans, which are then actually carried out by functional managers. Furthermore, the quality of the plans generated by the strategy matrix is likely to represent a significant improvement over those coming out of traditional planning systems. Given the interdisciplinary, multidimensional nature of the planning process associated with the strategy matrix, how could they not be an improvement?

The strategy matrix is particularly appealing to younger managers, who tend to resent finding themselves locked into authoritarian, hierarchical organizations. Furthermore, it is an excellent training device, suitable for the training of both junior and senior managers. The matrix approach also provides more individuals from technical or functional specialties with an opportunity to develop themselves into managers who are more broadly based. Finally, the strategy matrix allows for opportunities for personal growth and maturity that are not typically available within hierarchical organizations. Along with these increased opportunities for growth, the strategy matrix tends to stimulate more human energy and to place managers within an environment that is conducive to the creation of breakaway strategies.

Overview

Thus far, we have defined the strategy matrix as a multidimensional planning management system that is aimed at reducing some of the complexities associated with interdependent business activities. The two foundations on which the strategy matrix rests are strategic planning and matrix management. Basically, in its most succinct form, the strategy matrix is a matrix management approach to strategic planning. Therefore, in chapter 2 strategic planning is defined more explicitly in terms of forecasting the external environment and formulating objectives, goals, and strategies. This chapter also spells out some of the elements of matrix management and indicates how matrix management can be applied to problems of corporate strategy—including portfolio analysis, resource allocation, business strategy, and international management.

The next four chapters are concerned with specific applications of the strategy matrix to portfolio planning (chapter 3), to resource allocation (chapter 4), to business strategy (chapter 5), and to international management (chapter 6). The portfolio planning problem is concerned with which businesses the firm should be in, how they are to be financed, and with a limited number of top-down, corporatewide strategies. Chapter 3 begins with a critique of the so-called analytical portfolio models of The Boston Consulting Group and other management consulting firms. To illustrate the use of the strategy matrix with a portfolio of businesses, an example is described based on South Carolina Electric and Gas. Chapter 4 treats the problem of a resource allocation across a portfolio of businesses. Examples of the resource allocation matrix include Shell Oil, IBM, and Squibb.

In chapter 5, business strategy is defined from several different perspectives. The business strategy matrix is developed for Velsicol Chemical, Florida Power, and Federal Express. International management is the subject of chapter 6. Applications of the international strategy matrix include Dow-Corning, IBM, Alcoa, Dow Chemical, and Westinghouse. Chapter 7 summarizes some of the important practical, philosophical, and behavioral implications of the strategy matrix. For example, it considers the type of managerial philosophy and value system required to implement the strategy matrix. It also examines some of the implications of the strategy matrix on the attitudes of management toward life's meaning, business values, ethical principles, and corporate responsibility.

2

OVERVIEW OF THE
STRATEGY MATRIX

AS DISCUSSED in the introductory chapter, the strategy matrix is a multidimensional planning management system that was developed for the purpose of solving some of the complex problems that are generated by the highly interdependent nature of most business activities. Although the strategy matrix can be used for a variety of different types of planning—including strategic, project, and operational—and budgeting, we shall concentrate primarily on its use as a strategic planning tool. What differentiates the strategy matrix from other strategic planning systems is the fact that the planning function is organized as a matrix. Therefore, in the remainder of this book, whenever the strategy matrix is referred to, we shall mean a matrix management approach to strategic planning.

Matrix Management

Although matrix management has been used as a tool of project management since the 1950s, its use as a powerful conceptual framework for strategic planning wasn't recognized until it was introduced by Dow-Corning in 1968. Even then its potential as a strategic planning tool was hardly noticed by other companies. Not until the mid-1970s, when IBM, Intel, Shell Oil, and Federal Express began using it in their strategic planning, did the concept begin to take hold. Interestingly enough, the companies just referred to seem to have come upon the strategy matrix quite independently of each other—but precisely for the same reason, namely, as a means of maneuvering their highly interdependent business activities in a rapidly changing environment. Furthermore, most of these firms realized the similarity of their respective approaches to strategic planning only quite recently, 1984 to be precise, when their representatives met at a conference held at Duke University. Although there are now over a dozen major American companies using the strategy matrix, this has all happened relatively quietly, with little or no publicity or fanfare.

Most organizations, whether functional or divisionalized, are hierarchical in nature and are characterized by a one man-one boss chain of command. In a matrix organization, on the other hand, a multiple command approach to management exists in which there are two or more lines of authority. Although often considered to be a quite radical approach to management, critics of matrix management fail to recognize that most families, as well as the government of the United States, are examples of multiple command systems. Children are responsible to two authorities—the mother and the father—and so, coming up with solutions to family problems involving children usually requires negotiations between the child and the two parents. Similarly, the separation of the executive, judicial, and legislative branches of the U.S. government is a tripartite system of authority. This system of checks and balances is an integral part of our form of government and is a system that most Americans consider beneficial and necessary for preserving the rights outlined in our Constitution.

Aerospace and high-technology firms were among the earliest to employ matrix management. Nearly thirty years ago, they became cognizant of the need to give equal attention both to project management and to the management of the technical resources required to support these projects. Competitive pressures, combined with rapidly accelerating technological change, necessitated that these firms come up with a balanced view of the management of projects that draw upon common resources. A typical aerospace firm—Boeing, for example—routinely has a number of major projects going all the time. As was becoming more and more apparent to these firms back in the 1950s, there were obvious efficiencies to be gained from encouraging project managers to share their engineers and scientists as well as their sophisticated equipment. Because of the nature of the aerospace industry, decisions concerning project management and critical resource management must often be made simultaneously rather than sequentially. Trade-offs have to be made when project managers run up against resource constraints. Thus, the duality of projects and critical resources became increasingly apparent to industry executives as they responded to pressures both from the outside and from within their own organizations. Under these circumstances, a dual command system made eminent sense.

Another reason that motivated such companies as Lockheed, Rockwell, TRW, Control Data, and Intel to turn to matrix management was a simple case of information overload. Increased uncertainty concerning the external environment, complicated by an increased organizational complexity—which had been caused by the simultaneous diversification of products and markets—led to an increased need to both receive and generate information. Traditional hierarchical organizations found it increasingly difficult to respond to these information processing requirements. Stated alternatively, the interest in matrix management is merely a special case of society's need to replace hierarchical organizations with "networks." In his book *Megatrends*, John Naisbitt has expressed the need for networks in the following way:

. . . networks are people talking to each other, sharing

ideas, information, and resources. The point is often made that networking is a verb, not a noun. The important part is not the network, the finished product, but the process of getting there—the communication that creates the linkage between people and clusters of people.

Networks exist to foster self-help, to exchange information, to change society, to improve productivity and work life, and to share resources. They are structured to transmit information in a way that is quicker, more high touch, and more energy-efficient than any other process we know.[1]

Or, as Stanley M. Davis and Paul R. Lawrence put it in their book *Matrix*, if there is a high degree of uncertainty, complexity, and organizational interdependence, then conventional ways of processing information may break down:

If such a compound piling up of information-processing requirements were a rare, once-in-a-hundred occurrence, we could afford to ignore it. But it appears that this set of circumstances is to be the fate of more and more organizations, even in industries that we could label as stable and mature in the past. When organizations have come to terms with heavy information-processing loads, they have to open up and legitimate a more complex communications and decision network.

The matrix design, properly applied, tends to develop more people who think and act in a general management mode. By inducing this kind of action, the matrix increases an organization's information-processing capacity.[2]

ORGANIZATION STRUCTURE

Two concepts are basic to the structure of a matrix organization: a multiple command system and teams of people who are drawn from various subunits of the

Overview of the Strategy Matrix

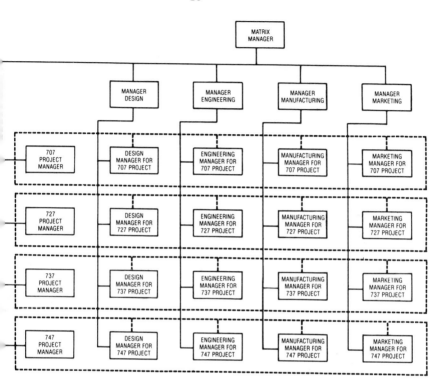

Figure 2-1

The Project-Resource Matrix for Boeing Aircraft Company

organization, thus cutting across one or more dimensions of the matrix. Figure 2-1 is typical of the prototype matrix organization used by aerospace and high-technology firms to manage projects and resources. For our example, we shall consider Boeing Aircraft Company, which, during the 1960s and 1970s, was involved in the design, engineering, manufacturing, and marketing of four different types of commercial aircraft. As figure 2-1 shows, there are four different aircraft projects—707s, 727s, 737s, and 747s—each of which shares a set of critical resources (design and engineering staff, manufacturing personnel and equipment, and marketing resources). Thus, the two dimensions of our example matrix are projects and resources.

Within the Boeing matrix, each project manager is responsible for a team of people who are drawn from all four resource organizations. A project team might include, for example, engineers, technicians, manufacturing specialists, and budget analysts. In addition, each project is assigned specific goals, operating plans, activities, resource requirements, schedules, budgets, and completion dates. All of these responsibilities fall within the purview of the project manager. Each project manager reports to the matrix manager who appointed him and who presides over both dimensions of the matrix. The principal challenge faced by the project manager is to secure the resources necessary to design, manufacture, and market the aircraft assigned to him and to do so according to schedules and budgets that have previously been negotiated and agreed upon.

Resource managers face a different problem. They must allocate the four resources efficiently across the portfolio of projects, doing so in such a way as to rationalize the competing goals of the four aircraft, each of which is competing for the same shared resources. The four resources denoted by the horizontal dimension of figure 2-1 are treated as cost centers. And, as such, their managers are charged with functional professionalism as well as with efficient resource allocation.

For the most part, Boeing's resources are organized to support the four aircraft projects. For example, within the engineering function, separate departments are assigned engineering responsibility for each of the four aircraft projects. Thus, the managers within this department have dual reporting relationships; that is, they report both to the vice-president of engineering and to the project manager for their particular project. The manager responsible for engineering for the Boeing 727, for instance, is responsible to the vice-president of engineering as well as to the Boeing 727 project manager. The same holds true for managers in the various design, manufacturing, and marketing departments.

Through dual reporting, the matrix enables management to achieve interfunctional coordination toward profit and growth goals without sacrificing functional professionalism or efficiency. The resource managers establish key functional standards of performance, make uniform planning assumptions, advise project managers on alternative resource programs, and prepare detailed cost-center budgets for approved projects. Although project managers are responsible to the general manager (figure 2–1) in terms of the management of their respective projects, they may also reside in one of the functional organizations and may be responsible to the head of that particular resource. Likewise, members of project teams have dual responsibilities to the project leader and to the manager of the resource in which they happen to be based. These dual reporting relationships represent the essence of the project-resource matrix. As can be seen in figure 2–1, the resource managers also report to the matrix manager. General guidelines for allocating the company's critical resources across the portfolio of projects are provided by this matrix manager, who may also serve as a referee to help resolve conflicts when negotiations between project managers and resource managers break down.

INFORMATION SYSTEM

As we have previously mentioned, project management of the type illustrated by our Boeing example will typically involve such activities as operational planning, scheduling, budgeting, accounting, and control. Special attention must also be given to motivation, reward systems, and employee compensation. However, implicit in the use of a multiple command system is the necessity of implementing a multidimensional (two dimensions in our example) management information system to support matrix management. If properly managed, a project-resource matrix should be supported by dual planning, budgeting, accounting, control, and reward systems. Since the strategy matrix is simply an extension of the concept of matrix management to an organization's strategic planning process, it will come as no surprise to the reader that the strategy matrix will also require a multidimensional management information system, a subject that will be covered later in chapter 7.

Overview of the Strategy Matrix

TEAM BEHAVIOR

The transition from a single-boss, single-command hierarchical organization to a multiboss, multicommand system made up of a group of interdisciplinary teams represents the single most important behavioral challenge of matrix management. Whether one is dealing with a project-resource matrix, a portfolio matrix, or an international matrix, the concept of teams operating within a multicommand, multidimensional structure represents the real core of matrix management. In our Boeing example (figure 2–1), each aircraft project manager is in charge of a team of people taken from within the ranks of the four resource organizations. Basically, the power within the organization is being shared between the resource managers and the project managers and their respective project teams. One of the challenges for the matrix manager who sits outside of the matrix and represents central management is the problem of achieving a balance between the two dimensions of the project-resource matrix.

Our purpose in describing matrix management in some detail has been to lay the necessary groundwork for applying the concept to strategic planning. In the remainder of this chapter, I will summarize some of the important elements of corporate strategic planning and indicate how matrix management can be used to organize the planning activities of a company to solve a number of specific problems of corporate strategy.

Strategic Planning Defined

The objective of strategic planning is to provide a process for the company's CEO and its various managers (business, critical resource, and international) that will enable them to make decisions today that will affect the company in the future and to do so in an environment characterized by a high level of risk and uncertainty. Strategic planning involves the formulation, analysis, and implementation of a set of corporate and business strategies that are consistent with the long-term goals and objectives of the firm in light of a set of assumptions about the firm's external environment. A strategy is a collection of activities to be carried out, either by corporate management, by the managers of individual businesses, or by the managers of the company's operations in a particular country.

External Environment

The initial step in the strategic planning process is for the company to generate a multiscenario forecast of its external environment. This forecast should include information about the economy, the behavior of competitors, government regulations, technology, international politics, and critical resources. I shall now summarize some of the important aspects of the risks and uncertainties in a company's external environment that must be projected at the outset of the strategic planning process.

ECONOMIC ENVIRONMENT

Heading the list of external factors affecting any company is the economic environment in which it must operate. For example, many corporate executives anticipated neither the 1974–1975 recession nor the one that dragged on from 1979 to 1983. Chrysler, Ford, and General Motors were among hundreds of corporate giants that paid a very high price for not adjusting their corporate strategies fast enough to cope with the rapid deterioration in the economic environment of these recessions. At neither time did the industry as a whole switch fast enough to smaller, more fuel-efficient cars to compensate for the rising cost of gasoline and thus avoid a significant reduction in sales and the resulting massive layoffs. In 1980, Chrysler tottered on the brink of bankruptcy for several months before being saved by a huge loan from the U.S. Treasury. Although General Motors did not introduce formal strategic planning until the late 1970s, as we have previously indicated, it turned to the strategy matrix in early 1984 to give it more flexibility in responding to changes in the economy, in the price of gasoline, and in the competitive environment.

Inflation, tight money, high-interest rates, and cash-flow problems are examples of other economic problems few firms managed to escape during the 1970s. The demise of Penn Central, Franklin National Bank, W. T. Grant, Penn Square Bank, and Baldwin-United did not go unnoticed by financial institutions, nor did the record number of bank failures in 1975 and 1984. Although inflation had subsided by 1983, other sticky economic problems reared their ugly heads: double-digit rates of unemployment, record federal deficits, and uncertainty about the repayment of loans from U.S. banks by Third World governments. For the very survival of the company in today's complex world, any strategic plan developed by a firm must include a set of assumptions about the relevant economic factors in the external environment.

COMPETITIVE ENVIRONMENT

The firm must also base its strategic plan on informed assumptions about the likely behavior of its leading competitors over the planning horizon. The plan must include reasonable assumptions about the answers to questions such as: Will a new firm enter the market? Will an existing firm lower its price or embark on a major advertising campaign? Will our product become obsolete as the result of a new offering by one of our competitors? How well are our most important competitors doing? What is the strategic plan of our principal competitor?

These are not easy questions, but a company's ability to compete successfully may be strongly influenced by the quality of its answers. With the high value of the dollar and increased competition from abroad, the competitive environment most American executives find themselves in today has greatly intensified from previous decades. Indeed, increased foreign competition was one of the most important factors that motivated Alcoa, IBM, and Westinghouse to adopt the strategy matrix for their international operations.

REGULATORY ENVIRONMENT

During the past fifty years, increased government regulation has become a fact of life not only in the United States but throughout the entire world, in capitalist and socialist countries alike. In the United States, no major industry has managed to escape the ever-extending arms of all levels of government. Although the Reagan administration has managed to reverse the trend toward increased government intervention into industry, government regulation remains a major source of uncertainty for many companies. Obviously, management must carefully monitor the social, political, and regulatory environment of the company in terms of pending legislation, changes in government regulations, and changes in public opinion. But all too often, American companies find themselves in the defensive position of merely reacting to legislation that has already been imposed upon them. An effective strategic planning process, on the other hand, enables management to anticipate changes in public opinion and thus to take effective action before public opinion pressures force legislation that may adversely affect the company's interests. The participatory nature of the strategy matrix is particularly conducive to the generation of effective ideas for dealing with the regulatory environment.

Velsicol Chemical introduced the matrix as a result of regulatory pressures imposed upon it by the Environmental Protection Agency. Squibb did so as a way of responding to Federal Drug Administration regulations. And IBM used the matrix as a way of meeting the regulatory challenges it faced from the U.S. Justice Department. Federal Express, on the other hand, has successfully used the matrix to take advantage of some of the benefits of airline deregulation.

TECHNOLOGICAL ENVIRONMENT

Changes in technology represent opportunities for some companies and threats to others. Technological change, then, should be viewed as another major source of uncertainty in the firm's environment. This is particularly true of high-technology firms such as computer hardware and software vendors, electronics firms, and electric utilities. IBM, Intel, and Federal Express are three examples of companies that adopted the matrix in order to provide themselves with the flexibility they needed to take advantage of rapidly changing new technologies. Because of serious technical and regulatory problems with nuclear power plants, electric utilities have literally been forced into formal strategic planning. Both Florida Power and South Carolina Electric and Gas have implemented the strategy matrix as a means of surviving in an era of technological uncertainty.

INTERNATIONAL ENVIRONMENT

Although the ability of OPEC to disrupt supplies and thus control the world price of crude oil has diminished in the 1980s, the potential for some form of political unrest remains in virtually every oil-producing country in the Middle East. Companies—including multinationals—that are heavily dependent on relatively unstable countries as their principal suppliers of raw materials must devote serious attention to long-term planning. By 1984, international political uncertainty was global in scope. U.S.-Soviet relations were at an all-time low, unrest was prevalent throughout Central America, and there was open warfare involving numerous countries in the Middle East.

On another front, however, the opening of trade doors to China represents a significant opportunity for companies that offer the type of goods and services China needs. This will be true both in the near future and in the longer term. It can be predicted that those firms that perceive the possibility of a new posture toward China and can position themselves to take advantage of the new situation may reap substantial profits. Recently, a few forward-looking American multinational corporations, such as Control Data and Westinghouse, have even proposed the possibility of East-West coventure companies as an alternative to a continuation of the arms race. Interest in this concept has been expressed by Western-oriented Hungarian companies such as Remix Manufacturing Company and BORSOD Chemical Company. Soviet and other Eastern European enterprises have also expressed interest in coventures with Western firms. Alcoa, Dow Chemical, IBM, and Westinghouse are some of the forward-looking American companies that have used the strategy matrix as a means of more effectively coping with global political uncertainty.

CRITICAL RESOURCE ENVIRONMENT

The decade of the 1960s was a period of rapid growth for most American companies. There were no supply constraints on corporate growth—merely limitations in the size of the market. But by the mid-1970s, American companies began facing a quite different external environment. For the first time since the end of World War II, industrial firms encountered serious shortages in a variety of different critical resources—natural gas, coal, petroleum feedstocks, and a broad range of minerals, to mention a few. Although the two recent recessions have brought temporary relief from these problems, an excessive rate of population growth worldwide and an increased per capita consumption among the affluent nations appear to be long-term problems. An additional cause of concern is the alarmingly high rate at which our natural resources are being depleted. Shell Oil's use of the strategy matrix, for instance, was strongly influenced by uncertainty about crude oil supplies and prices during the 1970s.

Goals and Objectives

Once a forecast of the company's external environment has been developed, the planning process focuses on the formulation of corporate objectives and goals, which, in the case of multibusiness corporations, must also be formulated for the individual businesses. Corporate *objectives* represent a general statement of the direction in which the senior management wants to see the company move over the long run. A corporate objective describes a future condition of the company toward which management can work. Objectives are usually descriptive rather than quantitative and do not have target dates for completion associated with them. They often represent a consensus of the company's executive committee about the long-term direction of the company. Objectives are likely to be strongly influenced by senior management's philosophy of business, including their personal values, sense of meaning, and attitudes toward corporate responsibility.

Many companies that use the strategy matrix have no formal objectives. There may be implicit objectives, however, that are understood by everyone within the company but that have never been written down. Northwest Industries, for example, does not delineate formal corporate objectives. However, the general managers of each operating company are provided with guidelines that they are expected to follow in preparing their strategic plans. The philosophy of Northwest Industries is, first, to operate in fields that are diverse and that are basic—in the sense that Northwest's products are commonplace and will always be purchased—and, second, to be the leader in each of these industries. In addition, corporate management stresses the importance of well-known brands in each field.

Hewlett-Packard's corporate objectives, on the other hand, represent an explicit statement of corporate responsibility for the company. The following seven objectives form the company's philosophy:

1 *Profit.* To achieve sufficient profit to finance our company growth and to provide the resources we need to achieve our other corporate objectives.
2 *Customers.* To provide products and services of the greatest possible value to our customers, thereby gaining and holding their respect and loyalty.
3 *Fields of Interest.* To enter new fields only when the ideas we have, together with our technical, manufacturing, and marketing skills assure that we can make a needed and profitable contribution to the field.
4 *Growth.* To let our growth be limited only by our profits and our ability to develop and produce technical products that satisfy real customer needs.
5 *Our People.* To help HP people share in the Company's success, which they make possible; to provide job security based on their performance; to recognize their individual achievements; and to insure the personal satisfaction that comes from a sense of accomplishment in their work.

6 *Management.* To foster initiative and creativity by allowing the individual great freedom of action in attaining well-defined objectives.

7 *Citizenship.* To honor our obligations to society by being an economic, intellectual, and social asset to each nation and each community in which we operate.

Whereas corporate objectives describe a future state of being for the company to work toward, corporate *goals* are more specific. They refer to a specific achievement to be realized within a definite time period. Goals are often quantifiable. Whether or not the senior management of a company will commit to specific numerical targets with dates associated with them is strong evidence of the degree of commitment management has for strategic planning. A strategic plan that fails to contain specific goals that are to be accomplished within a specific time horizon is a sham and is not likely to be taken seriously by anyone.

Corporate goals follow from corporate objectives. Once corporate goals have been defined, goals for specific business units and operating companies can be formulated. For instance, these from Florida Power might include (1) Achieve a specific return on investment each year for the next five years, (2) Increase revenues by a certain percentage by 1988, (3) Reduce employee turnover to less than some designated percentage by 1987, and (4) Reduce residential rates to a level that is in the lower half of the state's investor-owned utilities by a prescribed date.

Corporate Strategies

Once goals and objectives have been formulated and a set of assumptions about the company's environment is in hand, the problem of corporate strategy is fourfold: (1) portfolio analysis, (2) resource allocation, (3) business strategy, and (4) international management. Implicit in this definition of strategic planning is the assumption that the company's business activities can be subdivided into a number of not necessarily independent business units. I shall now define each of these problems in corporate strategy within the framework of the strategy matrix.

PORTFOLIO ANALYSIS

The portfolio problem involves three top-down decision problems: (1) Which businesses should the company be in? (2) How should these businesses be financed? (3) Which nonfinancial strategies should be employed across the portfolio of businesses and over different geographic locations?

The first of these problems is concerned primarily with merger-acquisition and divestiture decisions. The second problem addresses such issues as whether or not the company should use debt, equity, or retained earnings to finance its growth. And the third problem examines the possible use of a limited number of corporatewide, nonfinancial strategies that cut across business and international boundaries. An illustration of this third strategy might be a national advertising campaign devised by General Motors in which local dealerships run television spots that are identical to ones run by GM on the national television networks. Such a corporatewide strategy would assure a common image across the entire country. This effect would be impossible to achieve if each dealership organized its own unique advertising campaign.

The portfolio problem of corporate strategy can be formulated as a two-dimensional matrix whose dimensions are strategies and business units. But three different types of managers are associated with the portfolio matrix: a general manager, strategy managers, and business managers. The CEO is usually the general manager of the portfolio matrix and stands outside of the matrix. Both the strategy managers and the business managers report to this general manager. These corporate strategy managers formulate corporatewide strategies, such as acquisitions and divestitures, international marketing strategies, and long-term financial asset management. Strategy managers are also responsible for implementing their respective strategies in light of given corporate goals and objectives. Managers may come from either the corporate staff or from one of the businesses owned by the parent corporation. In the case of acquisition and divestiture strategies, as well as other corporate financial strategies, the strategy managers work almost exclusively with the corporate staff. However, corporatewide nonfinancial strategies require the cooperation and support of the general managers of the businesses for implementation. For example, a companywide advertising campaign will require the use of corporate resources and the resources of individual business units. National newspaper and television advertising can be handled at the corporate level, but local media advertising may necessitate the participation and support of managers of the relevant businesses.

The potential for conflict between corporate strategy managers and the general managers of the individual businesses is substantial. Since the existence of corporatewide strategies represents a potential loss of autonomy and control on the part of the managers of the businesses, the number of such strategies should be kept to a minimum. If they are not, the morale of the business managers may be severely compromised. Recall that in the case of Dow-Corning, since the business managers did not control the resources required to implement the strategic plans that they had formulated, they acted as coordinators for the implementation of these plans. The resources were actually controlled by the functional managers, not the business managers. Thus, the company had two-dimensional strategic plans, coordinated by the business managers, but ultimately implemented by the functional managers.

In the case of the portfolio matrix, we have strategic plans that are formulated by corporate strategy managers and then implemented by either corporate resource managers or business managers, or even both. Once again, the strategy managers who formulate the plans do not control the resources required to implement them. For example, a corporate strategy manager may be assigned a major acquisition. To implement this strategy, the manager may draw upon the talents of a variety of professionals on the corporate staff, such people as attorneys, accountants, financial analysts, and tax experts. Implementation of the strategy may also involve engineers and technical experts from within some of the business units. It is the strategy manager's job to coordinate all of these people through the entire acquisition process. Thus, although the strategy was formulated within a matrix, its implementation is ultimately achieved by coordinating a group of functional or resource managers.

The principal reason that firms such as South Carolina Electric and Gas (SCE&G) and Squibb have opted for the portfolio strategy matrix stems from the ability of the matrix to address problems of business interdependence. The matrix provides a means of organizing strategic planning activities. Prior to being reorganized as a holding company known as SCANA Corporation, SCE&G operated three major businesses: electric energy, natural gas, and urban transportation. It also operated several smaller businesses, and all of these were highly interdependent with regard to demand and shared resources. Conventional portfolio models of the type described in the next chapter make no sense because they essentially assume away the problem of interdependence. A functional approach to strategic planning also would not have adequately dealt with the problem of interdependence. Indeed, one of the major reasons that SCE&G found the portfolio strategy matrix appealing was that it helped break down some of the powerful functional barriers that were obstacles to interbusiness cooperation and function. The strategy matrix provided a rational way of attacking both the business interdependence problem and the zero-sum management style traditionally associated with electric utilities. In adopting the matrix, SCE&G management gained much more flexibility in responding to a rapidly changing environment. Employee morale improved as well.

The Squibb Pharmaceutical Group is another company that uses the portfolio strategy matrix to plan and manage its four interdependent pharmaceutical businesses. A rapidly changing competitive environment was a major contributing factor in Squibb's decision to implement the matrix. Since all four of its businesses—ethical, consumer, diagnostics, and animal health—had interdependent markets and manufacturing processes, again the alternatives open to Squibb were either the introduction of the portfolio strategy matrix or one or more forms of "muddling through," which, we have observed, usually means an attempt to pretend that the interdependence problem does not exist.

RESOURCE ALLOCATION

The resource allocation problem concerns itself with the level of commitment that is to be made to each business within the corporation's portfolio. With independent businesses, the only resource allocated across the portfolio by corporate management is cash. In the case of interdependent businesses, however, the company may allocate a number of different shared resources to specific businesses, including plant and equipment, raw materials, personnel, and research and development. The resource allocation problem may also be thought of as an investment problem or as a business-resource problem; that is, it poses the question of which critical resources should be invested in which business.

Three factors motivated Shell Oil to seek an alternative to traditional planning in the early 1970s—namely, the resource allocation strategy matrix. First, the entire petroleum industry was plagued by excess capacity in its petrochemical businesses. Second, OPEC's pricing policies in the Middle East had skyrocketed the price of crude oil. And third, all of Shell Oil's products and businesses were characterized by a very high degree of market and production interdependence. Standard divisional planning and capital budgeting techniques were incapable of sorting out the complex interdependencies of the petroleum industry in a timely enough fashion during a period of rapid change. The resource allocation strategy matrix offered Shell the flexibility necessary to handle the problems in a creative and profitable way, thus avoiding some of the "feast or famine" patterns that had been characteristic of the petroleum industry during the turbulent 1970s.

The resource allocation strategy matrix is two-dimensional, consisting of business units and critical resources. Both dimensions of the matrix are managed respectively by business managers and resource managers. Business managers are responsible for the overall performance of their businesses. They must obtain cash and possibly other resources, such as plant and equipment or personnel, from the resource managers of the parent company. Thus, business managers are in competition with each other for these scarce resources. Basically, their role in a matrix organization is one of interaction with resource managers and with other business managers.

The posture of business managers should be one of reason and advocacy. Through persuasion and negotiation, business managers attempt to obtain the necessary resources to achieve their goals and objectives. In some cases, critical resources may be in short supply, and so competing claims for these resources must be resolved by the general manager of all of the businesses and resources. While business managers must stand up for the needs of their individual businesses, they must also avoid the pitfall of overstating their cases. Often it is possible for effective business managers to devise cooperative solutions involving shared resources. The type of cooperative behavior required of business managers in a matrix organization does not come easily to managers who have been trained in a traditional hierarchical organization. But flexibility and adaptability are essential to the success of business managers in a matrix organization. Again, as was the case with the portfolio matrix, we have strategic plans formulated within the matrix format, coordinated by the business managers, but ultimately implemented by an entirely different set of managers who control most of the resources.

Perhaps the single most difficult obstacle to the implementation of the matrix stems from the fact that resource managers often lose power, status, and authority as the organization shifts from a single-boss style of management to a multiboss system. As the organization realigns itself, the resource managers must begin to share some of their traditional power either with strategy managers or with business managers. As their authority is divided among these other managers, resource managers may see themselves as less important and less powerful than they previously were. This morale problem is often exacerbated by the fact that the resource managers may increasingly have to confront subordinates who work for them but who also serve on strategy or business teams. For resource managers, who are accustomed to maintaining tight control over their subordinates, matrix management represents a serious threat, one that often leads to hostility and open resistance.

Over time, however, as a matrix organization matures, the resource managers often adapt to these changes and find them not only bearable but possibly even challenging. Even though it is the strategy and business managers who are the driving forces in a matrix organization, resource managers must still schedule and allocate resources across the portfolio of strategies and/or businesses. Within the matrix organization, resource managers still have many important activities. First, they must balance the needs of the different businesses and strategies in accordance with the goals and objectives of the organization. Second, they must schedule such resources as space, equipment, facilities, and maintenance. Third, they must oversee the training and administering of support staff, including clerks, secretaries, supervisors, and managers. Fourth, they must budget the company's critical resources in such a way so that the needs of the business and strategy managers are met. And, perhaps most important of all, to accomplish these goals with any degree of efficiency, the resource managers must balance work loads in such a way that, in terms of the demand for resources, excessive peaks and valleys are avoided.

The principal demand placed on resource managers by a matrix organization is flexibility. No longer does it make sense to adhere to some rigid, inflexible budget that may not even be consistent with the goals and objectives of the company. Resource managers, then, should assume a proactive role with regard to the business managers and anticipate changes in the work loads and resource demands of the businesses. Frequent negotiations must be initiated with the business and strategy managers when operating plans and schedules need modifying in response to changes in business conditions. For some resource managers, this new role is a bitter pill to swallow. For others, it is an opportunity. The experiences of Shell Oil, IBM, and Squibb will be used in chapter 4 to explore the resource allocation strategy matrix in greater depth.

BUSINESS STRATEGY

The problem of business strategy involves positioning a particular business unit in the marketplace and selecting the appropriate marketing, production, and organizational development activities to enable it to compete effectively. Whereas portfolio decisions are most often top-down decisions made by senior corporate executives, the selection of specific business strategies is usually a bottom-up decision. These business strategies can vary from simply introducing a new product into a new market to completely restructuring an entire industry, as we have recently witnessed in the steel industry in this country. The latter strategy, which was primarily triggered by U.S. Steel and LTV Corporation, consists of two major thrusts: closing inefficient plants and embarking on a wave of consolidations, all for the purpose of reducing labor costs and thus becoming more competitive in international markets. Continental Airlines used bankruptcy as a business strategy in order to freeze its unions in their tracks, reduce the number of employees by 50 percent, lower the cost per passenger mile by 25 percent, and significantly cut fares. On the other hand, Eastern Air Lines adopted a completely opposite business strategy in order to avoid bankruptcy. Eastern radically increased employee participation in ownership and management. That both of these airlines continue to operate today testifies to the flexibility and adaptability of the strategies employed by their management.

Since the business strategy matrix is typically applied to a single business rather than to a group of businesses, the principal issue for a company becomes the interdependence of specific functions and critical resources rather than interdependencies among businesses. Functional interdependence was a major problem at Velsicol Chemical, Federal Express, and Florida Power, three of the firms that began using the business strategy matrix in the late 1970s and early 1980s.

At the time the business strategy matrix was introduced at Velsicol Chemical, the future of that company was quite bleak. Indeed, most of the senior managers of the company had been fired as a result of the serious environmental and legal problems associated with the production and distribution of certain toxic chemicals. A completely new management team needed to be integrated into the company and done so in such a way as to minimize the interruption of ongoing business activities. Velsicol was a functionally organized business specializing in agricultural chemicals. To turn the company around, the new CEO required a high degree of flexibility in coordinating the interdependent functional activities and critical resources of the business. Solutions to many of the problems facing Velsicol required the use of strategies that demanded the cooperation of more than one functional manager. Because of the company's unique situation, strategic planning along strictly functional lines was totally out of the question. Although Velsicol remained a functionally organized company throughout the transitional period, it was necessary to superimpose a multidimensional strategic planning system across the functional departments, thus providing Velsicol with the flexibility it needed to return to profitability. Not only did the strategy matrix work for Velsicol, but it worked very, very well. Within three years from the time the business strategy matrix was introduced at Velsicol, the company had moved from the depths of despair to a position of record profitability.

Not only did Velsicol return to economic life with the use of the strategy matrix, but the entire corporate culture was essentially turned on its ear. The matrix helped Velsicol's new CEO transform the management style of the company from a heavy-handed, hierarchical, top-down approach to a more congenial, participatory, bottom-up style of management. Alienation and fear thus gave way to attitudes of cooperation and trust. Contrasting with the situation at Velsicol, from its very beginnings in the early 1970s, Federal Express has always been managed in a participatory, cooperative style. Therefore, it was not really surprising to learn that Frederick O. Smith had introduced the strategy matrix at Federal Express in the mid-1970s. Smith possessed the foresight to see that the matrix gave him the flexibility to introduce major new business strategies that would compete with the company's base business, namely, its overnight small-package operation. Federal Express has never experienced the problems of management alienation and political infighting that are so typical of most functional organizations. The matrix provided a tool for handling the functional interdependencies, while maintaining an attitude of cooperation and trust among the various functional managers. The phenomenal record of success at Federal Express speaks for itself.

The business strategy matrix employed by many of the firms we have discussed in this chapter involves the use, within a specific business, of business strategies that cut across the functional or resource lines of that particular business. The two dimensions of the business strategy matrix are, obviously, business strategies and resources. Business strategy managers operate within a single given business. They help formulate objectives, goals, and strategies that are consistent with the overall strategic plan of the business. They are also charged with coordinating the implementation of their respective strategies within the business. All of the resources needed by the strategy managers must be obtained from functional or resource managers within the business. Strategy managers come from within the existing functional or resource organizations, but they are responsible to the general manager of the business when it comes to the formulation and implementation of their particular strategies. As we have noted before, the duality of the matrix persists: matrix planning and functional implementation.

INTERNATIONAL MANAGEMENT

A fourth dimension of corporate strategy involves the management of multinational businesses. The strategic issues to be raised are similar to the ones we have observed at other levels of corporate strategy, but the issues become more complex as a company begins to cross national borders. The questions to be asked now include (1) Which businesses should be operated in which countries? (2) What strategies should be pursued in a particular country or countries? and (3) Which critical resources should be committed to which countries? Whereas applications of the matrix to problems of domestic strategy tend to focus on two-dimensional problems, international applications of the matrix may involve as many as four dimensions, including businesses, critical resources, strategies, and countries.

Thirty years ago, it was common for American companies doing business abroad to have 100 percent ownership of all of their foreign properties. When this was the case, the control of foreign investments was much more straightforward than it is today. Increased independence and nationalism, particularly among Third World countries, has considerably complicated the ownership pattern of foreign investments. In some countries, such as Cuba and Kuwait, the properties of American companies were nationalized outright. In other examples, the host country imposed various restrictions on the percentage of ownership permitted by a foreign investor. As a result of all these changes in the international business environment, a wide variety of ownership schemes and legal arrangements has emerged for the foreign investments of American-based multinational companies. These strategies vary, from firms assuming controlling interests and minority interests in foreign properties to the making of joint ventures, licensing agreements, and franchise arrangements. The political and legal rules of the game vary widely from country to country, depending both on the nature of the business and on the political stability of the host government.

THE CORPORATE STRATEGY MATRIX

The old rules for conducting business on an international scale simply no longer apply. A divisional planning process lacks the flexibility needed to keep on top of the complexities of this problem. Within a given country, there will typically be portfolio problems, resource allocation problems, and business strategy problems, all of which must be solved according to the legal, social, and political mores of that particular country. Under these circumstances, it is completely understandable why companies like Alcoa, Westinghouse, and Dow Chemical have introduced the multinational strategy matrix as a device for dealing with the enormous complexities of international management and strategic planning.

Although the applications of the portfolio matrix, the resource allocation matrix, and the business strategy matrix are fairly similar across different companies, this is not the case for the multinational strategy matrix. For Alcoa and Westinghouse, businesses and countries are the principal dimensions of their respective versions of the multinational strategy matrix. Dow-Corning and Dow Chemical, on the other hand, both use multidimensional strategy matrices for international management. Dow-Corning's multinational matrix includes businesses, countries, and critical resources, while Dow Chemical operates within a three-dimensional matrix consisting of six geographic areas, three major functions, and more than seventy major products.

Planning, budgeting, and implementing plans for the portfolios of business units that are organized by country are all responsibilities of country managers in multinational companies such as Alcoa and Westinghouse. These country managers can be likened to mini-CEOs who preside over subsets of the company's portfolio of businesses in foreign countries. Just as there may be companywide strategies, there may also be strategies that cut across regions or countries. This is one of the principal reasons that country managers usually have multiple bosses. For example, a country manager may report not only to a vice-president of international operations in the parent company's headquarters but also be answerable to those business managers whose businesses function in the particular country over which he has responsibility. Thus, country managers must not only interact with a number of business managers but possibly corporate resource managers and strategy managers as well.

The Off-Site Planning Meeting

An off-site meeting of the company's senior executives has been found by many of the firms that use the strategy matrix to be an effective way to launch the annual strategic planning process. Florida Power, South Carolina Electric and Gas, and Velsicol Chemical are three companies that have made successful use of an off-site meeting to initiate their planning process with the matrix. It is my belief that such meetings are valuable not only at the corporate level of a company but also at the operating company level. But regardless of whether or not the planning meeting focuses on the corporation or on one of its operating units, the meeting should begin with in-house staff experts presenting position papers on the state of the company and its external environment. These presentations—which should take no more than a half-day—might include an economic forecast, an evaluation of the company's financial position, an assessment of competition, and perhaps a review of the political environment. It should be the goal of these position papers to identify as clearly as possible the assumptions on which the company's strategic plan will be based.

Following the initial presentations, the next half-day is typically spent actually formulating corporate objectives or reviewing previous objectives. Usually an outside facilitator is called in to assist in the process of formulating objectives. The advantages of an outsider for this role are that the consultant brings to the meeting objectivity as well as experience with a variety of different companies. The formulation of corporate objectives is obviously a lot easier if the company already has a formal statement of its philosophy of management. If it does not, then it may want to consider devoting an extra half-day or so to the development of such a statement. The executives involved in the planning meeting should be clear in their own minds as to their company's philosophy of management before embarking on the objective-setting exercise. The meeting's participants should also keep in mind that the objectives they are formulating are corporatewide or objectives for an entire business, as in the case of an operating company like Velsicol. They are not at the meeting to formulate functional objectives.

The next half-day segment of the planning meeting should be devoted to the identification of corporate-wide goals or, in the case of a business unit, business goals. Again, an outside facilitator can make this process easier. However, I would like to point out that goal setting is a much tougher exercise than objective setting. The formulation of numerical targets —with dates attached on which these targets are to be accomplished—requires a much greater commitment from senior executives. If these two tasks of objective setting and goal setting are attempted without first finding agreement on the company's philosophy of management, repressed conflict among senior managers may occur. The facilitator, of course, must anticipate these eruptions of temper and discord and be able to handle them with tact and sensitivity.

Once objectives and goals have been formulated and agreed upon, the group can then turn its attention to corporatewide strategies (in the case of the company as a whole) or to individual business strategies if an operating company like Florida Power is the focus of the meeting. Strategy formulation usually also requires about a half-day of work. The entire off-site meeting normally occupies about two to three days of time.

The off-site meeting should generate the following three documents: (1) a review of the company's environment, (2) a preliminary statement of the company's objectives and goals, and (3) an initial description of the major strategies the company or business intends to pursue.

Immediately following this off-site meeting, the CEO of the company, or the general manager of the operating company, should appoint strategy managers who will be responsible for tightening the definitions of the strategies to which they have been assigned. They should also indicate which goals and objectives will be impacted by their respective strategies. In essence, strategy managers are expected to refine the objectives, goals, and strategy definitions that came out of the formulation process. For each strategy, they should prepare a strategic plan that includes not only objectives, goals, and strategic activities but also a notation of major resources required to implement the strategy. Strategy managers should also come up with an analysis that rationalizes the strategic actions in light of the given goals and assumptions about the firm and its environment. The intention of this analysis is to support the assertion that the strategies being proposed will, indeed, yield the desired goals and that this assertion is based on given assumptions about the external environment. Lastly, the strategy manager, whether at the corporate level or the business unit level, is responsible for coordinating the implementation of the strategy.

Analysis

A strategic plan is void of meaning unless it also includes some form of *analysis* to support the assertion that the proposed strategies are capable of yielding the desired results (goals and objectives) given the accepted assumptions about the firm's external environment. Absence of serious analysis in a strategic plan is clear evidence that it probably is merely an academic exercise that will not be taken seriously by anyone. The analysis that appears in a strategic plan should be based on more than just one scenario about the company's external environment.

Throughout the 1970s, corporate strategic decisions were analyzed through extensive use of two analytical tools: portfolio models and business simulation models. As we noted in chapter 1, however, portfolio models are often inappropriate when there is a high degree of interdependence among businesses. For this reason, we shall now briefly examine business simulation models as an alternative analytical tool.

Business simulation models not only possess the ability to simulate the effects on corporate or business unit performance of alternative portfolio strategies, they are also useful for evaluating alternative resource allocation, business unit, and international management strategies. The portfolio models are limited primarily to problems of portfolio analysis. Business simulation models, on the other hand, can handle interdependent business units and interdependent functions of single business units, thus providing much more analytical power and flexibility than can be generated with portfolio models.

Most companies utilizing the strategy matrix include some type of computer-based planning model for evaluating the effects of alternative strategies on corporate or business unit performance. Many planning models are programmed for use on large mainframe computers, but more recently this kind of analysis is also being done on microcomputers. Nearly all of these computer-based planning models were developed with the aid of some high-level planning language such as EXPRESS, FCS, or IFPS. The term *decision support system* has come into vogue to describe the computer software required to do planning modeling in an interactive, conversational mode. With these decision support systems, it is now possible to develop interactive models of individual business units, models that recognize the interdependence of such areas as finance, marketing, and production. With some software systems, it is also possible to consolidate the business plans produced by each of the business planning models of a particular company either vertically or horizontally. Decision support systems for microcomputers are also available now. Software packages like LOTUS 1–2–3 make it possible for very small businesses to produce cost-effective pro forma financial plans to evaluate the effects of different strategies. IBM, Squibb, Federal Express, and Shell Oil all use computer simulation models to support their use of the strategy matrix.

I am introducing computer-based planning models here simply to note that they have become a very important part of the analytical support of strategic planning. Not only are such models useful for strategic planning in divisional and functional organizations, they are also essential to the analytical support of the strategy matrix. More will be said about the role of decision-support systems with the strategy matrix in chapter 7.

Implementation

The general manager of a matrix organization shoulders the ultimate responsibility for the implementation of the goals and objectives of each arm of the matrix. In the case of Dow-Corning, the matrix manager is the president of the company, and both business managers and functional managers report to him. At Shell Oil, an executive vice-president plays a similar role. Power balancing, management of information flow, and enforcement of goals and objectives are among the important functions of the general manager of a matrix organization.

It cannot be overly stressed that careful attention must be given to the power and authority delegated to each arm of the matrix. In single-boss hierarchical organizations, this is obviously not an issue because lines of authority are clearly delineated from top to bottom. However, in a matrix organization, the power balancing becomes more complex. For example, in Dow-Corning's strategy matrix, it would make little or no sense to give total authority to the functional managers and let the business managers fend for themselves. Considerable attention must be devoted to power balancing in the early stages of the evolution of a matrix organization. This is particularly true at times when it is necessary to shift the power balance from one dimension of the matrix to another.

Matrix organizations generate substantially more information than do functional and divisional ones. It is the responsibility of the matrix manager to assure that this information flows in a fashion as flexible and informal as possible.

In functional and divisionalized companies, there are two types of individuals who are legitimately entitled to do strategic planning: the CEO and the line managers. Planning can only be effectively carried out by those people who are personally responsible for implementing plans and for achieving the goals and objectives set forth by the strategic plans. One of the major features of the strategy matrix is the fact that it broadens the base of participation in the planning process and puts the responsibility for strategic planning in the hands of those who are actually responsible for implementing the plan. And, as we noted earlier in this chapter, it does all of this at a much deeper level within the organization than was heretofore thought possible. As we have also previously mentioned, strategy managers and business managers are responsible only for the coordination of the implementation of plans with the strategy matrix. However, their strategy teams and business teams usually include people brought in from the resource organizations that will be directly involved in the implementation of strategies and business plans. Therein lies the real power of the strategy matrix. When strategic planning is tied to a matrix-type organization structure, one moves away from the ivory tower atmosphere of the centralized corporate planning staff toward where the action actually takes place: the arena of the line managers. Indeed, one of the greatest strengths of the strategy matrix is that it closes the gap between planning and implementation.

3

PORTFOLIO ANALYSIS: WHICH BUSINESSES SHOULD WE BE IN?

IN THIS CHAPTER, we shall be discussing the first of the four problems of corporate strategy, namely, portfolio analysis. Each of the following three chapters will, in turn, address one of the other problems of corporate strategy: resource allocation, business strategy, and international management. In each chapter, we shall define the problem, indicate why conventional approaches to the solution of the problem don't work, reformulate the problem using the strategy matrix, and then use examples and case studies to illustrate the experience of various companies with the matrix in solving their particular problems.

As mentioned before, in order for a firm to have a portfolio problem, it must be possible to subdivide its business activities into a collection of strategic business units, which may take the form of divisions, operating companies, or even subsidiaries. According to General Electric—one of the first companies to adopt the strategic business unit (SBU) concept—an SBU displays the following characteristics:

> . . . a unique set of competitors, a unique business mission, a competitor in external markets (as opposed to internal supplier), the ability to accomplish integrated strategic planning, and the ability "to call the shots" on the variables crucial to the success of the business.[1]

SBUs have been defined around specific products, markets, and technologies, as well as around the personal interests of particular managers. Therefore, it is difficult to be very precise as to how any particular SBU is defined. Furthermore, it is fairly common within many corporations for internal political considerations to dictate the definitions of SBUs. Although these definitions can be quite arbitrary, as was the case with General Electric's computer business, the economic consequences of how the SBUs are defined can come back to haunt a company many years later.

Portfolio Strategies

The portfolio problem of corporate strategy is concerned with three highly interdependent issues. First, the question of just which businesses (SBUs) should be included in the corporation's portfolio must be asked. This is followed by the second critical question, which is "How should these businesses be financed?" And, third, the firm will want to ascertain whether or not there are certain nonfinancial strategies that cut across the entire portfolio of businesses. If there are, then it must be determined if they are of sufficient importance to the corporation as a whole that they should be managed at the corporate level rather than at the business unit level. Implicit in this definition of the portfolio problem is the assumption that the parent corporation acts not only as the portfolio manager but also as the banker for the various businesses in the portfolio. Depending upon the degree of independence and autonomy among its businesses, the corporation may allocate cash and possibly other resources—such as critical raw materials—to the businesses. Now let's elaborate on each of the three portfolio problems that were defined in chapter 2.

ACQUISITION AND DIVESTITURE STRATEGIES

When growth through increased sales became increasingly difficult in the 1960s and 1970s, many companies embarked upon a strategy of growth through mergers and acquisitions. In the case of large international oil companies with huge cash reserves, for instance, acquisitions looked like an attractive alternative investment opportunity in light of shrinking options in exploration and development. Among the strategic questions that had to be asked were "Should the company seek acquisitions?" And "If so, what should the nature of these acquisitions be?" Alternatively, if not, then "Should the company divest itself of specific businesses?"

Among the larger conglomerates active in the merger-acquisition binge of the last twenty years have been General Electric, ITT, Tenneco, United Technologies, and Rockwell International. As I have indicated before, many of the mergers that occurred within the past ten to fifteen years were strongly influenced by the philosophy of portfolio planning developed and popularized by The Boston Consulting Group and by McKinsey and Company. Some of these acquisitions led to financial success. Others were more problematic, such as Exxon's experience with Reliance Electric, Warner-Lambert's investment in Entenmann's, Sohio and Arco's plunge into the copper industry, Mobil's experience with Montgomery Ward, and GE's by-the-book acquisition of Utah International. Later in this chapter, we will examine the philosophy underlying The Boston Consulting Group's approach to merger-acquisition analysis and point out some of its inherent limitations, for it is this, I believe, that has motivated some firms to consider the strategy matrix as an alternative way of dealing with portfolio problems.

FINANCIAL STRATEGIES

Given a portfolio of businesses, each with its own business plan, the second matter of strategic concern to the senior management of a company is the question of how to finance the portfolio of businesses. For most multibusiness companies, the corporate treasurer acts as the banker to the individual businesses; that is, he serves as the principal financial strategist of the company. As such, the treasurer is concerned with primary financial questions. For instance, the treasurer wants to determine if acquisitions to the portfolio should be financed through the sale of equity, the issuance of debt, or the retention of funds generated internally by the firm. He will also ask: "Should a particular business be managed for long-term or short-term cash flow?" These are among the important financial strategies associated with portfolio management. Financial strategies of this type usually involve evaluating the impact of alternative financial decisions on liquidity, financial leverage, and dividend policy.

NONFINANCIAL STRATEGIES

During the heyday of the merger-acquisition movement of the 1960s and 1970s, corporate-level strategic planning for multidivisional companies was restricted to purely financial strategies of the type described above. Nonfinancial corporate strategies were discouraged by management as being inconsistent with the spirit of decentralization. Strategic planning, other than corporate financial planning, was viewed as an activity exclusively in the control of the general managers of the individual business units. However, by the end of the 1970s, awareness that perhaps some operating companies had actually been given too much autonomy and latitude in defining business strategies increased. Some operating companies, it was realized, were not only behaving in a manner inconsistent with the values and objectives of the parent company, but they were also failing to take advantage of certain synergies between the operating companies.

Consider the case of the pharmaceutical industry. Twenty years ago, there was a wide variance from country to country in government regulations regarding advertising, testing, and disclosure of information for new drugs. It was not uncommon for American drug companies to vary their standards widely from one country to the next when they introduced new pharmaceutical products overseas. However, pressure from the American public and the U.S. government has caused most of the leading American drug companies to standardize their new product strategies. The standards of quality for such products are now uniform globally even though they often far exceed the requirements of some Third World countries. Thus, although these pharmaceutical companies are highly decentralized, they have implemented new product strategies that are common to all of the countries in which they operate.

IBM's global emphasis on customer service and excellence represents another type of corporatewide strategy that cuts across all business and profit centers throughout the world. However, it is good to be reminded every so often that if the corporation wants to maintain the morale and motivation of its individual business managers, the number of strategies to be managed on a top-down basis by the corporation should be limited. If the business managers feel that they have little influence over the strategies affecting their respective businesses, then morale will suffer at the business unit level.

Alternative Approaches to the Problem

Since World War II, major American companies have used three alternative approaches to deal with the problem of portfolio analysis: divisional planning, portfolio models, and the portfolio strategy matrix. Prior to the 1970s, many decentralized companies, such as General Motors, Monsanto, and AT&T, did little or no corporate strategic planning whatsoever. Each division or operating company was run as a fully autonomous unit and did its own strategic planning. As recently as the mid-1970s, the senior management of Monsanto disclaimed any interest at all in corporate strategic planning. It was the general managers of the operating companies of Monsanto who held sole responsibility for strategic planning. At General Motors, the five automobile divisions were run as independent fiefdoms, receiving little or no guidance from corporate management. And, at AT&T, the situation was similar; the regional operating companies seemed to be functioning independently of parent company control.

What we saw during the era of large-scale decentralized operations in this country was that most of the strategic planning that did take place was essentially bottom-up strategic planning. So, given that there was virtually no top-down strategic planning of the type we are now discussing taking place in the corporate headquarters, it is not surprising to discover how little attention was devoted to the so-called portfolio problem. The CEO made portfolio decisions, often with only minimal consultation with the general managers of the operating units of the company and with limited information and virtually no formal analysis. For the most part, these large companies used relatively primitive techniques in evaluating the trade-offs of investments and alternative businesses. Indeed, there was no one on the corporate staff who possessed the analytical skills to do this type of sophisticated analysis.

In one sense, the divisional approach to strategic planning pretended to deny the very existence of top-down portfolio planning problems. At the very best, the divisional approach could only be used to address the portfolio problem indirectly. On the average, however, the divisional approach to strategic planning actually did deny the existence of the problem. Thus, by introducing analytical portfolio models into American companies in the late 1960s, The Boston Consulting Group presented a response to the complete vacuum in planning at the top of most American corporations. It was realized by business analysts, finally, that decentralization had gone entirely too far, that the behavior of many corporations was bordering on complete irresponsibility toward the activities of their operating companies. In some cases, corporate executives almost seemed to prefer to remain in a state of ignorance about their operating divisions rather than attempt to come to grips with some very sticky problems related to trade-offs among investments and alternative businesses.

The portfolio models described in the following sections were, clearly, superior alternative methods for approaching portfolio analysis because the divisional approach to portfolio planning was, in reality, no alternative at all. A clearly defined need existed for top-down strategic planning, and so the portfolio models of the 1970s represented an attempt to fulfill that need. However, as we have previously noted in chapter 1, and shall spell out in greater detail in the following section, these relatively simplistic planning tools have not proven to be the panacea that many thought or hoped they would be. Limitations in portfolio models, as well as the problems we have noted in divisional planning, have given rise to the use of the portfolio strategy matrix as an approach to portfolio planning that overcomes the limitations of each of these previously used approaches.

Portfolio Models

A collection of techniques known as *portfolio models* evolved during the late 1960s and early 1970s. These came about in response to the vacuum that existed in many firms as to their ability to analyze corporate portfolio problems, particularly the merger-acquisition problem and the problem of financing a portfolio. Developed originally by The Boston Consulting Group, these techniques have been widely emulated by McKinsey and Company, Arthur D. Little, Strategic Planning Associates, and Marakon Associates, to mention only a few of the management consulting companies that use this approach to portfolio analysis; such models are also closely identified with General Electric Company and the Harvard Business School.

The principal advantage of portfolio models is their simplicity. However, as we have previously noted, serious problems arise when companies attempt to apply these tools to interdependent businesses or to nonfinancial portfolio strategies, which most of these models completely ignore the possibility of. The portfolio strategy matrix described at the end of this chapter represents an attempt to overcome some of the limitations of these portfolio models. But, to illustrate some of the important features of portfolio planning models, it may be useful to review in some detail The Boston Consulting Group model, an approach that rests on two relatively simple concepts: the growth-share matrix and the experience curve.

GROWTH-SHARE MATRIX

The portfolio problem of the firm can best be expressed as a problem of balancing the cash flows among alternative businesses. That is, the excess cash generated by low-growth businesses is used to support those high-growth businesses possessing a perceived strong market potential, while eliminating businesses with low market potential that do not generate significant cash flows.

The Boston Consulting Group has suggested

four guidelines for determining the cash flow of a business:[2]

1 Margins and cash generated are a function of market share. High margins and high market share are correlated.
2 Growth requires cash input to finance added assets. The added cash required to hold share is a function of growth rates.
3 High market share must be earned or bought. Buying market share requires an additional increase in investment.
4 No business can grow indefinitely.

The payoff from growth must come when growth slows, or it never will. The payoff is cash that should not be reinvested in that business. With the growth-share matrix, precisely where a business falls in a two-dimensional matrix of market growth and market share and where it might fall in the future may have significant strategic implications for corporate resource allocation, business strategies, and management recruiting strategies. The growth-share matrix illustrated by figure 3–1 assumes that the activities of the company have been subdivided into strategic business units, each of which is separable from the others. For each business, the *market growth rate* and the *market share* are plotted on the growth-share matrix. The definition of *market share* employed by The Boston Consulting Group is based on the concept of market dominance, which is just the ratio of the company's market share to the market share of its largest competitor. This emphasis upon the largest competitor springs from the relative cost implica-

Market Share

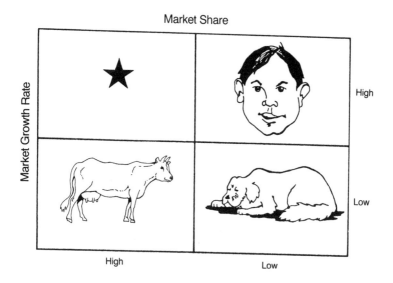

Market Growth Rate

High

Low

High   Low

Figure 3–1

Growth-Share Matrix

SOURCE: The Boston Consulting Group

tions of The Boston Consulting Group's theory that the firm with the largest market share will often have the greatest accumulated experience and therefore the lowest unit costs.

The second dimension of the growth-share matrix is a measure of business attractiveness. As used by The Boston Consulting Group (BCG), this measure of business attractiveness is the market growth rate, which is defined as the annual rate of growth of sales in constant dollars. Increased sales growth is often associated with economies of scale, reduced unit costs, and an improved competitive position, and it is for this very reason that sales growth was chosen by the BCG over some other measure of business attractiveness. Frequency of purchase of products, market concentration ratio, barriers to entry in the market, size of the market, and structure of the market were measures passed over in favor of the straightforwardness of market growth rate.

The growth-share matrix in figure 3-1 is divided into four quadrants: cash cow, problem child, star, and dog. The boundaries separating these quadrants are to some extent arbitrary, with the market growth boundary usually set at 10 percent and the market share boundary at 1.5 times the market share of the largest competitor. Of course, it is possible to define a growth-share matrix with a finer grid than the one used by The Boston Consulting Group, but its four quadrants will serve nicely enough to illustrate the basic concept of the growth-share matrix.

Cash Cow. Businesses with high market share and slow growth frequently generate large amounts of cash, more than is required to maintain market share. But the excess cash generated by such businesses should not be reinvested in these businesses. For, if the return on investment (ROI) is greater than the market growth rate, then the cash cannot be reinvested indefinitely without reducing the ROI. The appropriate strategy is, therefore, to protect the current position of the cash cow while generating cash to invest in selected stars, problem children, research and development, and other long-term projects.

Problem Child. The upper right-hand quadrant of figure 3-1 represents a business characterized by high market growth and low market share. The problem child has an inferior market position and typically requires additional investment. If cash is not provided, a problem child may fall behind and drop out of the market. However, even if cash is provided, the business may turn into a "dog" when the growth slows. Problem children require large injections of cash to buy market share; they often become liabilities unless they can be transformed into market leaders.

A good illustration of a problem child situation comes from the case of General Electric. Apparently the company's decision to get out of the computer industry was based heavily on analyses that showed that its computer business was a problem child with little hope of becoming a star. Given the competition from IBM, there was little chance of reversing GE's prospects in this area without massive amounts of additional cash. GE was simply not willing to take such a large risk and so opted to sell its computer business to Honeywell.

Star. Here we find the high growth, high market share business. Stars usually show positive profits but may or may not produce positive cash flows, depending on the level of additional investment that is required by the business. If the star remains a market leader, then it will eventually evolve into a cash cow: growth is reduced, and reinvestment requirements decline.

Dog. Businesses with low market share and slow growth are called "dogs." Although these companies may show a positive profit, that profit must consistently be reinvested simply to maintain market share. Dogs are worthless. They are evidence of the business's failure to achieve a position of market leadership or to cut its losses when faced with a "no win" situation.

In summary, the growth-share matrix represents a conceptual framework on which portfolio investment decisions can be based. A balanced portfolio of businesses calls for, first of all, heavy investment in stars, whose high share and high growth assure the future. Protection of cash cows is also required in order to generate funds for further growth. The third tactic associated with the growth-share matrix involves selective investment in problem children, those with potential for being converted into stars. And, finally, this BCG matrix calls for the liquidation of dogs.

EXPERIENCE CURVE

The *experience curve* is the second concept on which the portfolio planning methodology of The Boston Consulting Group rests.[3] As can be seen from the experience curve shown in figure 3–2, the assumption is made that there is an inverse relationship between the unit costs of manufacturing a product and the accumulated output or experience associated with the production of that product. According to the BCG, unit costs (in real terms) decline approximately 20 to 30 percent each time accumulated experience is doubled. The literature abounds with examples of businesses to which the experience curve seems to apply. Such businesses tend to have relatively stable

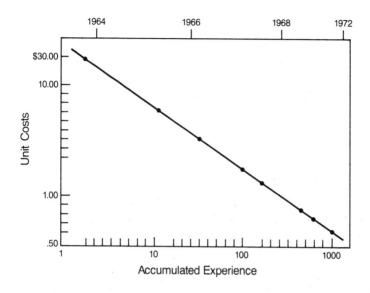

Figure 3-2

Experience Curve for Integrated Circuits
SOURCE: The Boston Consulting Group

markets in which the competitor with the dominant market share acts as a price leader, and the slope of the experience line is approximately 70 to 80 percent, indicating that prices will decline 20 to 30 percent each time accumulated output doubles. Semiconductors, crushed limestone, gas ranges, polyvinylchloride, steam turbine generators, and automobiles are all examples of businesses that seem to display this type of experience effect. However, many economists find it difficult to accept the fact that all experience curves seem to slope downward and to the right, implying ever-decreasing costs. In the world of microeconomic theory, cost curves eventually turn back up after an initial decline. Included among the economic factors thought to explain the experience effect are increased labor productivity, additional education and training, changes in technology, economies of scale, and substitution of one factor input for another.

Bruce D. Henderson, the founder of the BCG, has derived a number of strategic implications from the experience curve on topics ranging from growth, market share, product design, and debt capacity to make or buy decisions and procurement negotiations.[4] For example, the BCG seems to have almost unlimited faith in increased market share as a means of increasing profits for a business. Some economists would suggest that businesses should not only look at market share but also at the relationship between incremental costs and incremental revenues before embracing increased market share as some kind of panacea. On the other hand, Henderson's statement that "costs will decline proportionately faster or slower when cost elements are shared between more than one business," is difficult to challenge.[5] Unfortunately, he does not offer any specific advice on how to integrate these shared costs. Indeed, this is one of the major shortcomings of the entire BCG approach.

FINANCIAL STRATEGIES

One of the most interesting aspects of the BCG approach to portfolio planning is the way in which the growth-share matrix and the experience curve are jointly used to formulate corporate financial strategies.[6] To the extent that growth is perceived as a critical measure of corporate performance, then the role of finance takes on considerable importance. The company that grows the fastest is the company that generates enough cash to add to its assets at the fastest rate. According to the BCG, a company that grows the fastest is a company that sustains the highest rate of return on equity. Such a firm confronts its competitors with the greatest force of resources as well. The BCG has shown analytically that a firm's sustainable rate of growth depends in part on, and is limited by, the rate at which it can generate cash flow for commitment to the growth target, and the return it expects to earn on these funds. The sources of these funds are, of course, retained earnings, debt, and new equity. The rate of return and the risk profile of alternative businesses will determine their effectiveness. The important thing is to sustain the optimum mix of strategic resources in the right place at the right time and in the proper amounts.

The role of chief financial officers in the BCG approach is to oversee the development of a set of financial strategies and policies that are consistent with each company's goals and objectives. It is also their responsibility to help develop financial opportunities to achieve these goals. To do this, chief financial officers must clearly understand the intricacies of the financial parameters that contribute to their company's growth and the consequences of their manipulation.

Financial strategy is an integral part of the company's overall portfolio strategy and must be linked to the company's cost position and competitive environment. Financial strategy must necessarily be based on the following interdependent set of variables: (1) debt policies, (2) dividend policies, (3) price policies, (4) industry growth, and (5) competitive cost positions. The Boston Consulting Group's approach offers two guidelines for integrating financial strategy, competitive strategy, and portfolio selection. First, a business must generate either growth or cash in order to remain in the corporate portfolio. And, second, businesses with high growth will use more cash than businesses with low growth.

In conclusion, financial strategy is an important element in a company's collection of portfolio planning tools. It is by no means limited to the simplistic use of debt combined with the avoidance of dividend payments. It does mean, though, that a portfolio of businesses must be created to maximize debt capacity and overall cash generation ability. Redirection of cash flow into areas of opportunity such as new ventures, acquisitions, and others, should also be an integral aspect of financial strategy. The net effect of financial strategy, then, is a continual postponement of corporate maturity, combined with increased earnings in mature businesses, minimum profit margins in growing businesses, and maximum financially sustainable growth.

SUMMARY

The entire BCG approach to the portfolio problem can be summarized as follows: today's growth should be taken from the *stars* (high share, high growth).

Stars are typically almost self-financing, but care must be taken not to allow other competitors to erode market share. On the other hand, today's financing should be taken from the *cash cows* (high share, low growth). All stars eventually become cash cows when the growth slows and share is maintained. But tomorrow's growth should be taken from the *problem children* (high growth, low share). A problem child, unless it attains high market share, will never supply cash or meaningful growth. Problem children require heavy funding to attain high share while growth remains. Finally, nothing worthwhile can be expected from *dogs* (low share, low growth). Divestiture is the recommended strategy.

OTHER PORTFOLIO MODELS

Although the BCG approach to the portfolio problems of corporate strategy is by far the most widely used approach, we shall briefly summarize other alternatives—particularly the GE-McKinsey screen. (Each of these portfolio models assumes that the company has been divided into SBUs.) When McKinsey and Company subdivided General Electric into forty-three SBUs in the early 1970s, it also introduced the company to a variant of the growth-share matrix known as the *GE-McKinsey screen* (figure 3–3). Each SBU is represented by a three-by-three matrix, the dimensions of which are *relative market strength* and *industry attractiveness*. Relative market strength is a weighted average of such criteria as market share, product quality, manufacturing costs, and relative profitability. Industry attractiveness is a weighted

McKINSEY

INDUSTRY ATTRACTIVENESS

	High	Medium	Low
High	Invest	Growth	Earnings
Medium	Growth	Earnings	Harvest
Low	Earnings	Harvest	Divest

RELATIVE MARKET STRENGTH

Figure 3–3

The G.E.-McKinsey Screen

SOURCE: General Electric Company

average of overall market criteria such as market size, market growth, and industry profitability. Each SBU is characterized as having either high, medium, or low market strength and industry attractiveness. Depending on where a particular SBU falls in the matrix, it should either *invest* capital for *growth*, hold by balancing *earnings* and cash use, or *harvest* or *divest*.

Competitive position and *industry maturity* define the dimensions of Arthur D. Little's (ADL) equivalent to the growth-share matrix. ADL's competitive position is analogous to McKinsey's relative market strength. Businesses are classified as to whether their competitive positions are dominant, strong, favorable, tenable, or weak. On the other hand, industry maturity is based on the concept of product life cycle. Industries are categorized as embryonic, growing, mature, or aging. Where the particular SBU falls in the ADL matrix determines the appropriate strategy recommendation.

As a result of the success of The Boston Consulting Group in attracting clients in the field of strategic planning, three former associates of Bruce Henderson at the BCG started their own consulting firm to work in the field of corporate strategy. These spin-offs of the BCG include Bain and Company, Braxton Associates, and Strategic Planning Associates (SPA). Not surprisingly, their approaches to the portfolio problem closely parallel that of the BCG. The most recent entrant into the field of portfolio planning consulting is Marakon Associates, a firm proposing that the appropriate philosophy of management is one in which the company is run to "create value for the shareholders." Emphasis is placed on managing the company's portfolio to maximize the value of the company that depends on equity cash flow as well as the cost of equity capital. Value is said to be created when sustainable return on equity exceeds the cost of capital, thus resulting in a market-to-book ratio in excess of one. For a given spread between return on equity and the cost of capital, investment growth magnifies the creation of value, provided that the spread is positive. A negative spread will result in the destruction of value. At the SBU level, spread and growth typically compete with each other:

1 Growth strategies sacrifice spread
2 Spread strategies reduce growth
3 Exception: highly successful product differentiation

Whether to sacrifice spread for growth or vice versa depends on the terms of the trade-off.

BENEFITS

In chapter 1, we noted that a relatively high percentage of the largest companies in the United States are using portfolio models. That so many of them have used such models over the past decade for strategic planning provides substantial evidence that the models must contribute something of value to the strategic planning of these firms. First, portfolio models represent a relatively simple way of showing the trade-offs associated with investments in alternative businesses. Second, the graphic nature of these illustrations makes them easily understood by nontechnical senior executives. Third, the models are useful in assessing the financial consequences of alternative portfolio strategies. Fourth, management's understanding of the relationship between the firm and the market is improved when such models are used. Fifth, portfolio models are ideal expository devices for teaching strategic planning in graduate schools of business and in executive development programs.

Limitations of Portfolio Models

Throughout the 1970s and into the early 1980s, the portfolio models of the type described above became relatively standard tools for analyzing corporate portfolio problems. However, during the past few years, the adequacy of these models to cope with corporate portfolio planning problems has increasingly been called into question. At first blush, the exact definition of a particular strategic business unit may not seem all that important. Pragmatic considerations might dictate that we formulate some rough guess as to how to subdivide a company into business units. Unfortunately, as was illustrated previously by the example of General Electric, the implications of ill-defined SBUs can result in serious consequences on corporate performance many years later. Strategic business units that are based on particular markets may also raise some further methodological issues. Often it is very difficult to define and quantify market share for certain industrial markets. Unlike consumer goods, which lend themselves to the use of survey research, market share for industrial products frequently eludes precise measurement.

All of the portfolio models so far discussed assume that SBUs have independent production processes and demand functions. However, Jerome M. Waldron has shown that firms that treat interdependent businesses as though they were independent can be expected to overprice their products and underproduce, thus resulting in lower profits than would have been the case had the interdependence been taken into consideration.[7] This phenomenon is caused, in part, by the failure of interdependent businesses to take advantage of the "economies of scope" that occur in situations where the total cost of producing two or more products in combination is less than the cost of producing each product separately. It is also possible to show that the stock market can be expected to undervalue the shares of firms that have interdependent demand functions. Furthermore, as we have indicated before, if the demand functions of two or more businesses are interdependent, then it is literally impossible to define the concept of a growth-share matrix or a GE-McKinsey screen, for example. Thus, we no longer have a single growth-share matrix for a specific business, but, rather, an infinite number of growth-share matrices, the exact number depending on what the demand situation is in the other interdependent businesses impacting on the business in question. In such a situation, simplistic concepts like the growth-share matrix may provide management with a completely distorted view of the profitability and long-term strategic implications of specific businesses. For now, management must not only worry about the effects of competing products in the marketplace but also about competing products offered by other businesses in the parent company's portfolio.

In addition to the problems of obtaining cost accounting data and market share data for the growth-share matrix and the experience curve, portfolio models also experience problems in forecasting the future values of market share, market growth, and unit production costs. A final limitation to consider is that all of the portfolio models are essentially static models, which makes it relatively difficult for them to adjust to rapid changes in the firm's external environment. Every growth-share matrix and every experience curve is based on very explicit assumptions about the economic, competitive, critical resource, and regulatory environments of the firm. Any changes in the external environment must be reflected in the tools of analysis we are using.

The Portfolio Strategy Matrix

In response to many of the serious shortcomings of divisional planning and portfolio models, a special case of the strategy matrix known as the *portfolio strategy matrix* has recently evolved. Designed specifically to overcome the lack of flexibility of portfolio models in dealing with interdependent businesses, the portfolio strategy matrix works in this way. Assume that a company possesses a portfolio consisting of several businesses, some of which have interdependent production processes and/or demand functions. Although each business has its own strategic plan developed by its general manager, it must also function with reference to a limited number of corporatewide strategies that are managed at the company level and that cut across the different businesses. These corporate portfolio strategies may include acquisition-divestiture strategies, financial strategies, and nonfinancial strategies.

As we indicated in chapter 2, the corporate strategic planning process begins with a review of the company's environment. Corporate goals and objectives should then be formulated by the company's executive committee, which should consist of the CEO, the vice-president of finance, the vice-president of planning, and the general managers of three or four of the company's principal businesses. Once goals and objectives have been identified, the executive committee should next formulate a set of, say, six or eight corporate strategies. An example of such a strategy might consist of the acquisition of a specific new business to be added to the company's portfolio. Alternatively, the search for certain types of businesses to be considered as merger-acquisition candidates could also be treated as a strategy. Divestiture of a poorly performing business would be another possible corporate strategy. On the financial side, taking the company public and offering a new issue of common stock could also be considered a portfolio strategy. Refinancing the company's debt structure is another example of a financial strategy. A companywide marketing or advertising campaign, on the other hand, is a typical nonfinancial portfolio strategy. Given the fact that some or all of the businesses in the company's portfolio are interdependent, each of these potential strategies must be evaluated in light of its possible effects on each of the businesses in the portfolio as well as on the company as a whole.

Having defined a set of corporatewide portfolio strategies, the executive committee should then designate the strategy managers who will be responsible for fine tuning the strategies and for implementing them. Each strategy should have its own manager and team responsible for formulating a more complete definition of the strategy. This same team would also coordinate the implementation of the strategy once it receives final approval from the executive committee. These teams should consist of perhaps a half dozen people, some of whom are on the corporate staff and some who come from the key businesses.

Over a four-to-six-week period, each strategy team should carry out a logical sequence of activities. The team should first review the strategy definition and propose to the executive committee any changes that seem appropriate. Once the final definition is approved, the team should then identify the particular corporate goals and objectives that will be impacted by the implementation of the strategy. The team's third step should be to determine the major resource requirements necessary to implement the strategy: money, human resources, equipment, space, and so on. An analysis—based on alternative scenarios in the firm's external environment—should then be conducted in order to evaluate the effects on the target goals and objectives of implementing the strategy. For example, the strategy might be analyzed under a base case scenario as well as on optimistic and pessimistic scenarios, as we described in chapter 2. If either the strategy or the resource requirements need to be adjusted in order to reflect either the optimistic or pessimistic scenarios, then this fact should be noted in the analysis.

The result of this process is a strategic plan unique to each specific strategy. To ensure, however, that the interdependencies among strategies and businesses are adequately considered, strategy managers should meet as a group at least weekly, optimally under the leadership of the vice-president of planning. At the end of the four-to-six-week period, the strategy managers should each present their plans to the executive group for review and approval. Once all of the strategies have been finally accepted, it is then possible to begin formulating the overall corporate strategic plan, which should be viewed as preliminary until the bottom-up plans of the businesses have been approved and a final consolidated strategic plan produced. The point to emphasize here is that the corporate portfolio strategies are expected to impact the strategic plans of the individual businesses. This is why the corporate planning process must precede the planning process of the business units.

What is being asserted in the above discussion is that strategy teams not only replace portfolio models, but that use of such teams will eventually reduce the number of expensive outside consultants required to formulate, evaluate, and implement portfolio strategies. When strategies are formulated by the same teams that will have responsibility for implementing them, the tasks of strategy formulation and implementation become linked much more closely than is usually the case in hierarchical organizations.

The portfolio strategy matrix is capable of dealing with the interdependencies among strategies and among businesses in two different ways. First, the strategy teams enable the planning process to expand, both in breadth and in depth within the company. Since team members are recruited from line organizations as well as from the corporate staff, more information is available about the business and strategy interdependencies than is usually the case with the top-down portfolio models. Second, teams may choose to utilize either business simulation models or an overall corporate planning model when they evaluate the effects of alternative strategies. However, as we pointed out in chapter 2, simulation models are much more flexible than the naive portfolio models since they are capable of incorporating data relative to the interdependencies among businesses and strategies.

The information content, as well as the information processing power of the strategy teams, gives the strategy matrix an overwhelming advantage over top-down portfolio models. An additional strength of the matrix is that more people from deeper within the organization become involved in formulating the major decisions that affect the future of the company. The psychological benefit of increasing the number and level of managers who contribute to the creation of the company's strategies is enormous since there will be an increase in the number of people who will take these strategies very personally, something they themselves intimately identify with. Before long, the strategy teams learn to play the role of the outside consultants. They can take credit when ideas work, but if they submit ill-conceived strategies, then they have the responsibility of implementing their mistakes. Thus, with the strategy matrix, strategies assume a very personal significance for those involved in creating them.

To assure itself that the portfolio strategies are being implemented properly, the executive committee should insist on quarterly review meetings with the strategy managers. Again, we must emphasize that the key element in the strategy matrix is the fact that the strategy formulators and the strategy implementers are one and the same.

To illustrate the application of the portfolio strategy matrix, we will consider the case of SCANA Corporation, the parent company of South Carolina Electric and Gas Company. SCANA began using the portfolio strategy matrix in 1982, adopting it in order to meet a number of objectives. The company wished to absorb the organizational effects of a merger, to bring its nuclear plant into commercial operation, to accomplish some of its goals in terms of rate relief, and to convert an oil-burning generator into a coal-burning generator.

SCANA Corporation

SCANA Corporation is an electric and gas utility holding company that owns wholly twelve subsidiaries. One of these is South Carolina Electric and Gas Company (SCE&G), which is a multibusiness utility primarily concerned with the generation, transmission, and distribution of electric power and the transmission, distribution, and sale of natural gas. SCE&G also renders an urban transportation service in both Charleston and Columbia, South Carolina. The company's annual sales are over $1 billion.

Within its service area in South Carolina, SCE&G provides electric service to approximately 357,000 customers in 115 towns and surrounding areas. Electricity is provided at wholesale to five cooperatives, to one public power body, and to three municipalities for resale. It also provides natural gas to more than 186,000 retail customers. This natural gas is sold at wholesale to eleven resale customers, who then distribute it at retail. SCE&G also operates more than 1,600 miles of gas transmission lines in its service area.

In addition to SCE&G, SCANA Corporation owns eleven other companies (figure 3–4): (1) South Carolina Fuel Company, which acquires, owns, and provides for SCE&G's nuclear and fossil fuel requirements; (2) South Carolina Pipeline Corporation, which engages in the purchase, transmission, and sale

117

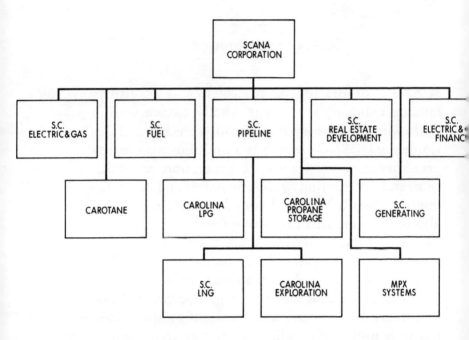

Figure 3–4

Organization Chart of the SCANA Corporation

SOURCE: SCANA Corporation 1984 Annual Report

of natural gas on a wholesale basis and in direct industrial fuel sales; (3) South Carolina Real Estate Development Company, which holds and develops pres-
ently held real estate; (4) South Carolina Electric and
Gas Finance, which obtains funds outside the United
States for financing activities of SCE&G and its affili-
ates; (5) Carotane, which engages in the purchase, delivery, and sale of propane gas at retail; (6) Carolina
LPG Corporation, which engages in the pipeline

transportation of propane; (7) Carolina Propane Storage Corporation, which stores propane; (8) South Carolina Generating Company, which owns and operates Williams Station (a power plant) and sells electricity to SCE&G; (9) South Carolina LNG Company, which owns and operates liquefied natural gas storage facilities; (10) Carolina Exploration, which engages in the exploration and development of natural gas; and (11) MPX Systems, which engages in digital transmission service (fiber optics).

The reason for going into so much detail in describing the twelve businesses of SCANA Corporation is to reinforce the fact that these businesses are highly interdependent with regard to transmission lines, pipelines, fuels, personnel, service equipment, and service areas. It would be impossible to disentangle these twelve businesses and have any single one of them operate as a stand-alone business. Given the extent to which the corporation's resources are shared and the fact that gas and electricity are direct substitutes, the portfolio models described earlier in this chapter could never even be seriously considered by SCE&G or SCANA.

When I began consulting with SCE&G in 1981, the company had just acquired a new CEO, Virgil C. Summer, and had just completed a major reorganization. The company's earnings had been relatively flat over recent years, and company morale was not very high. The original game plan we considered for SCANA called for the design of a divisionalized planning process focused on the company's three major lines of business—electric energy, natural gas, and urban transportation. A functional strategic planning process within each of the three major divisions was also envisioned. However, the limitations of this approach soon manifested themselves. Among other factors, the three principal businesses shared a number of common resources, including finance and accounting, marketing, human resources, legal services, and engineering support.

Midway through the development of the divisionalized planning process, CEO Summer decided to merge SCE&G with Carolina Energies, a nearby natural gas utility. The purpose of this merger was to strengthen SCE&G's top management, which in turn precipitated yet another major reorganization within the company. As a result of these reorganizations, it became more and more apparent that the divisional approach to strategic planning simply would not work for SCE&G. The functional interdependencies among the three major lines of businesses were too numerous even to attempt serious strategic planning along divisional lines unless some way could be found to take the interdependencies into account. For the reasons stated earlier in this chapter, portfolio planning models were never seriously considered as a viable alternative in a situation such as this. An additional complication generated by the recent merger was the problem of integrating the management and staff of Carolina Energies into SCE&G. As with most other utilities, a functional line separating the various departments within the company had been drawn, which discouraged cooperation among functional managers. During this same period, construction of its first and only nuclear power plant was nearing completion, which meant that the company would soon face the tedious, resource-consuming tasks of preparing the plant for commercial operation and licensing by the Nuclear Regulatory Commission, as well as obtaining rate relief from the Public Service Commission in order to recover its enormous investment in the plant. And finally, to further emphasize the complexity of the situation faced by SCE&G, the company was also in the process of converting one of its oil-fired power plants into a coal-fired power plant, which was no trivial undertaking.

The longer I worked with Summer, the more apparent it became that not only was he interested in using the planning process to take control of the company, but that he also saw it as an opportunity to begin changing the corporate culture. Most electric utilities are notorious for their inflexible, bureaucratic, and rigid organization structures, and they are usually managed in a highly militaristic, top-down, authoritative style. From the very outset, Summer signaled his desire to change SCE&G's management philosophy to one more participatory in nature. He also opened the ranks of the senior officers of the company to women and blacks, a move heretofore unprecedented in the industry, particularly in the southeastern part of the United States.

Given these signals and the openness of Summer to the possibility of changing the corporate culture, I described to him some of the experiences of Shell Oil, Federal Express, and Velsicol Chemical in implementing the strategy matrix as a means of addressing some of their problems. Somewhat to my surprise, Summer decided to scrap our plans for a divisionalized planning process, and we began work immediately in 1982 on the implementation of the strategy matrix at SCE&G. The strategy matrix stood out as the only conceptual framework capable of containing all of the complexities and interdependencies of SCE&G's businesses simultaneously.

The corporate restructuring of South Carolina Electric and Gas Company was completed on December 31, 1984, and included the formation of SCANA Corporation, a holding company with twelve subsidiaries. This structure offered several benefits to SCE&G's investors and stockholders, for it allowed the company to separate its existing businesses into distinct but related companies that reflected the varied operating requirements, risks, markets, financing needs, and growth opportunities of these activities. It also enhanced the company's financial flexibility. When financing is required, it can now be done either by SCANA Corporation or by its subsidiaries, thereby enabling each corporation to design securities tailored to the specific risks involved or to its investors' requirements. The new structure provides the financial and organization flexibility necessary to meet the changing economic environment for electric and gas utilities. The strategy matrix was extended to SCANA Corporation in 1985.

The planning process begins each spring at SCANA with an off-site conference attended by members of the planning team. Senior officers of SCANA, SCE&G, and some of the more important subsidiary companies are all members of the planning team. Approximately twelve of these planning team members control the principal resources of SCANA Corporation, including cash, nuclear operations, fossil operations, gas and electric transmission systems, and human resources. This meeting begins with presentations from the planning support team, whose reports take the form of multiscenario forecasts of SCANA's internal and external environments, including the economy, government, technology, critical resources, consumer attitudes, and human resources. Based on the current environmental assessments that have just been given, the planning team then reviews the company's objectives, goals, and strategies. For the' most part, these do not change very much from year to year. There were nine objectives included in SCANA's 1985 strategic plan; these covered such topics as finance, the nuclear plant, customer satisfaction, human resources, image, sales, efficiency, corporate development, and communications. (It is interesting to note that one of the 1984 objectives for SCE&G called for the adoption of a corporate structure to pursue business opportunities in new and changing environments. The strategy to implement that objective included the creation of the SCANA Corporation.) Associated with each of these objectives is a set of corporatewide goals, such as achieving certain financial targets by 1987 and increasing natural gas sales by 3 percent each year.

To achieve these corporate goals, the planning team of SCANA formulates a set of corporatewide strategies that cut across SCE&G and the other eleven businesses owned by SCANA. In this case, a corporate strategy refers to a set of activities aimed at achieving corporatewide goals and objectives, and they fall into one of two categories. Most of these strategies represent activities that are above and beyond the scope of routine operations and have planning horizons that exceed one year. Others, however, do encompass routine operations, but are of such potential importance to the company that they are raised to the level of corporate strategies to assure top management's continuous attention. The operation of the company's nuclear power plant falls into this latter category of activities.

SCANA's planning team identified ten corporate-wide strategies for 1985. These are summarized here:

1 *Customer Satisfaction.* Earn improved customer attitudes by increasing employee awareness and by aggressively addressing sources of dissatisfaction.
2 *Communication.* Develop, through a system of actions, an environment that promotes effective internal and external communication.
3 *Image.* Achieve a desirable perception from all constituencies by projecting a "we-care" attitude.
4 *Marketing/Sales.* Consistently achieve the goals of a realistic, customer-oriented marketing plan through an aggressive, coordinated sales effort.
5 *Rates.* Meet the requirements of dynamic markets and lower unit costs for the company's utility businesses by implementing new and innovative rate structures and pricing mechanisms.
6 *Human Resources.* Implement meaningful human resource programs to address corporate and employee needs through more effective supervisory and management development.

7 *Productivity.* Attain a more efficient and productive organization through increased employee awareness and involvement, improved work control systems, and recognition of productivity achievements.

8 *Technology and Business Development.* Improve the company's ability to evaluate new technologies and business opportunities by developing its technical resources and organization.

9 *Environment.* Develop an approach to identify critical environmental issues and the resources necessary for practical solutions through an environmental coordinator and team.

10 *Nuclear.* Effectively utilize the resources, through training and compliance with regulatory requirements, to operate and maintain the company's nuclear plant in a safe, reliable, and efficient manner.

SCANA Corporation's portfolio strategy matrix is illustrated by figure 3–5. It shows the ten corporate-wide strategies that cut across SCE&G and the other eleven businesses of SCANA Corporation. Although SCANA uses the portfolio strategy matrix for its long-term strategic planning, neither SCE&G nor any of the other eleven operating companies of SCANA is organized as a matrix. Rather, all are organized along functional lines; indeed, most of SCANA's resources are still controlled by the senior functional officers of SCE&G. For this reason, it may be useful to include an alternative view of SCANA's strategy matrix, which we do in figure 3–6. In this strategy-resource matrix, we notice that the ten strategies of SCANA not only cut across twelve different businesses but that they also share a common set of critical re-

SCANA CORPORATION

BUSINESSES

Figure 3–5

Portfolio Strategy Matrix for SCANA Corporation

SOURCE: SCANA Corporation

sources, including electrical generating capacity, the electrical distribution system, natural gas supplies, the natural gas distribution system, fossil fuels, nuclear fuels, human resources, and cash. These critical resources are controlled by resource managers, most of whom maintain their positions in the lead utility, namely SCE&G. In combination, figures 3–5 and 3–6 illustrate the fact that SCANA's ten strategies are highly interdependent in terms of their effects on the twelve businesses and the utilization of the company's shared resources.

126

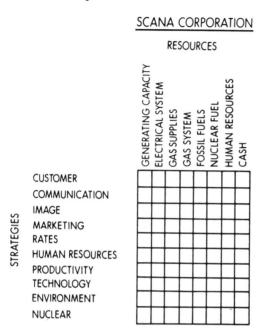

SCANA CORPORATION

RESOURCES

Figure 3–6

Strategy-Resource Matrix for SCANA Corporation
SOURCE: SCANA Corporation

Each of the ten 1985 strategies was assigned its own strategy manager and a strategy team, whose members are selected from different businesses and functional areas. Strategy managers must negotiate the resources required to implement their strategies from the functional vice-presidents of SCE&G and the other operating companies of SCANA. The managers then put together a three-page strategic plan for their particular strategy. These plans include a strategy description, a list of objectives, goals, resource requirements, an analysis, and contingency plans.

127

With assistance from the company's computer-based planning models, the effects over a five-year period of the ten strategies are evaluated on the basis of three different scenarios of the external environment. The strategy managers then present their respective strategies to the planning team for evaluation and review. After revision, if necessary, and final approval by the planning team, the strategies are consolidated and further evaluated as an integrated strategic plan. Quarterly review meetings are held with the strategy managers to evaluate the progress that has been made on implementation of the strategies. These review meetings are an extremely important part of the entire strategic planning process since they provide feedback to the strategy managers from the CEO and the planning team.

The strategy matrix at SCANA also drives the annual operating plans and budgets of SCE&G and the other eleven operating companies. Operational planning and budgeting are organized along functional lines within each operating company since the functional managers who control the critical resources are the ones ultimately responsible for implementing all the strategic plans. The functional managers of each of the twelve operating companies must rationalize their operating plan and budget in light of the company's corporatewide goals and strategies. Specifically, resource managers are expected to allocate resources in a manner that is consistent with the corporate strategic plan.

Although SCANA is divisionalized into twelve operating companies, each of which is organized along functional lines, its strategic planning process is based on a two-dimensional matrix that consists of ten strategies and twelve businesses. Strategic planning is a team effort involving strategy managers, resource managers, and business managers. Although resource managers carry out the operating plans required to implement the corporate strategies, the coordination of strategy implementation is the responsibility of the strategy managers. As is always the case with the strategy matrix, we have a matrix-oriented strategic planning process combined with the implementation of strategic plans by functional managers.

There are four major reasons that the senior management of SCE&G (and more recently SCANA) opted for the use of the portfolio strategy matrix as a strategic planning tool. First, the matrix provided a means of dealing with the company's three highly interdependent, primary businesses—electric power, natural gas, and urban transportation. The BCG-type portfolio planning models were not a realistic alternative because of the limitations that were noted earlier in this chapter. Second, the matrix provided a means of coping with functional interdependence within the individual operating companies thus influencing SCE&G's decision to adopt the matrix. Not unlike the situation at other utilities, this was a particularly serious problem at SCE&G, where the functional boundaries seemed to have exacerbated the sense of competitiveness among functional officers. Third, the matrix gave the company much needed flexibility in responding to rapid changes in its external environment. Fourth, the matrix improved morale by broadening the base of participation in important corporate decisions. Over one hundred managers, including some of the younger, more promising ones, now participate in the company's strategic planning process.

By year end 1983, SCE&G had already reaped substantial benefits from its new approach to strategic planning. Its nuclear power plant was licensed by the Nuclear Regulatory Commission and was brought into full commercial service. In addition, the Public Service Commission approved the inclusion of the nuclear plant in its rate base. An imaginative early retirement program was implemented. The company received a clean bill of health from a management audit mandated by the Public Service Commission. The conversion of an oil-fired power plant to a coal-fired power plant was nearing completion. The company's earnings per share increased by 10 percent, and the company was given an improved bond rating. And one last benefit to note is that SCE&G increased its quarterly dividend. Not bad for a firm in an industry that is overwhelmed by problems!

The company's success continued through 1984, another year of record earnings. In 1984, earnings per share jumped to $3.05 per share by comparison with $2.29 per share in 1983. These results were influenced by 1983 rate-case decisions. Among the 1983 strategic planning efforts that bore fruit in 1984 were the accreditation of nuclear training programs, implementation of the company's first comprehensive marketing plan, increased attention to productivity, and more than 250 employee recommendations for improvements through the employee idea program. Marketing was placed at the forefront of SCE&G's corporate strategy in 1984 with the implementation of the company's first formal marketing plan. Results have already become visible in some areas. Transit losses have decreased following the implementation of marketing strategies to increase charter service and revise routes. In addition, industrial sales goals for natural gas and electricity have been exceeded.

Conclusions

At one level, any attempt to compare the portfolio strategy matrix with the analytical portfolio models of The Boston Consulting Group or McKinsey and Company is a lot like comparing apples and oranges. The two approaches differ so radically that we must resist the temptation to oversimplify such a comparison. Portfolio models represent a relatively narrow view of the portfolio planning problem, which is restricted to the financial aspects of the company's portfolio decision problem. Based on a very restrictive set of assumptions about the independence of SBUs, these planning tools attempt to provide some quantifiable rules of thumb for making financial portfolio decisions. Basically, the approach is rational and analytical, with a heavy emphasis on quantification. The analysis involved in using these tools is typically done by outside consultants who work directly for the CEO of the company. The whole approach is quite consistent with top-down, hierarchical strategic planning.

Fundamentally, the portfolio strategy matrix differs from the BCG approach in two important ways. As we have shown, a portfolio strategy matrix provides a convenient conceptual framework for incorporating interdependent business units. The BCG approach cannot touch the degree of flexibility offered by the strategy matrix in terms of handling interdependent businesses. In addition, unlike the portfolio models of the BCG, the strategy matrix invites a participatory approach to strategic planning by drawing a large number of managers into the strategic planning process. It is not an elitist planning tool custom-designed to feed the ego of the CEO. Rather, the strategy matrix welcomes the opinions and expertise of a broad range of managers. It is a bottom-up planning tool that encourages cooperation and trust among the managers of various business units. In many ways, the management philosophy underlying the use of the strategy matrix is completely antithetical to the isolationist, secretive management style associated with those executives who make top-down portfolio decisions in isolation and without consulting the parties affected.

Another characteristic differentiating the portfolio strategy matrix from the portfolio models described in this chapter is its ability to process an enormous amount of information. The two-dimensional growth share matrices and experience curves of the BCG provide only a minimum amount of information to senior management for making decisions. The strategy matrix, on the other hand, generates much more information and has the added capability of processing this information. Indeed, one of the challenges of the portfolio strategy matrix comes from reducing all of this information into a meaningful form suitable for decision making.

Further differentiating the strategy-matrix approach to the portfolio problem from the BCG approach is that it is much more qualitative. This is an important distinction in light of the increasing realization that graduate schools of business may have gone overboard in their advocacy of narrowly defined quantitative techniques for managerial decision making. Portfolio planning problems do not lend themselves to analysis via simple two-dimensional diagrams or the optimization of whatever measure of financial performance is currently in vogue. The strategy matrix ensures a qualitative approach to a complex problem. While it can provide the same types of information available through the use of analytical portfolio models, it does so with a great deal more information as well.

The analysis that underlies most of the portfolio models described in this chapter is usually done by expensive outside consultants. In contrast, the portfolio strategy matrix, strategy formulation, evaluation, and implementation are all carried out by strategy teams that closes the gap between strategy formulation and implementation and reduces the need for outside consultants. Furthermore, the participatory nature of the portfolio strategy matrix often improves morale and broadens the experience base of middle managers by enabling more of them to become involved in strategy formulation and implementation. Finally, unlike the static portfolio models, the portfolio strategy matrix is a dynamic planning process that can increase the company's flexibility in responding to a changing external environment. For example, whereas many electric power companies seem virtually frozen in their tracks as a result of the changing regulations of the Nuclear Regulatory Commission, SCE&G, through the use of the matrix, has remained sufficiently flexible to bring its nuclear station successfully on line.

Ultimately, the portfolio strategy matrix treats the problem of portfolio planning as a problem of planning a network of interconnected businesses in which the interdependencies are met head on throughout the planning process. The matrix does not attempt to ignore business interdependencies. Rather, it exploits this interdependence in such a way so that the entire company gains. Thus, creative networking is used to replace the naive isolationism of traditional portfolio planning.

4

RESOURCE ALLOCATION: WHAT LEVEL OF COMMITMENT SHOULD WE MAKE TO EACH BUSINESS?

THE SECOND PROBLEM of corporate strategy is the whole question of resource allocation; that is, determining what level of commitment the corporation should make to each of the businesses in its portfolio. In the case of a conglomerate such as ITT, in which its telecommunications equipment business, its bakery, and its international chain of hotels are essentially independent of each other, cash is the only resource that corporate management allocates across the port-folio. The subject gets more complex when interde-pendent businesses become the focus of attention. Integrated oil companies, utility holding companies, pharmaceutical companies, and computer manufac-turers, to mention only a few, are all kinds of firms that share certain critical resources, such as crude oil, plant and equipment, real property, and research and development. For these firms, the corporate invest-ment decision may include the allocation of a number of different resources in addition to cash to the indi-vidual business units.

Obviously, major investment decisions will influ-ence any solution to the company's portfolio prob-lem. That is, acquisitions and divestiture decisions as well as corporate financial strategies depend heavily on the financial commitments necessary to support the businesses in the company's portfolio. Although the final approval of major investment decisions such as a new plant, the introduction of a new product, or a large commitment to R & D are usually made by cor-porate management, these decisions are based on in-formation gleaned from the strategic plans that have been provided by the individual business units. Since they are an integral part of the bottom-up strategic plans developed by the general managers of the indi-vidual operating companies or business units, invest-ment decisions are, by their very nature, decisions that are negotiated between corporate management and these general managers.

To come to grips with the corporate resource allo-cation problem, two different approaches were used in the 1970s, one of which—the portfolio models—was discussed in chapter 3. Now we shall turn our attention to the other approach that enjoyed great favor in the last decade—that of capital budgeting techniques. Although portfolio models were developed primarily in response to the problem of portfolio analysis, they have also been applied as guidelines for making resource allocation decisions among businesses in a company's portfolio. While these analytical tools remain popular in many quarters, for all of the reasons cited in chapter 3, we now know that they are simply not up to the job of handling resource allocation problems among interdependent businesses. Portfolio models are incapable of processing and analyzing all of the relevant information that is required to evaluate interdependent businesses. Not only are misleading results often produced, but entirely incorrect strategies can all too easily be generated. Capital budgeting techniques, on the other hand, have often offered an alternative approach for evaluating investment decisions.

Capital Budgeting and the Strategy Matrix

CAPITAL BUDGETING

Suppose, for example, that an individual business unit proposes to build a new plant that will produce a major new product to be introduced into the marketplace. The general manager of this business would like to obtain from the parent corporation the funds with which to finance the new product and the new plant. To support the case for corporate funding of this project, a financial analyst prepares a forecast of the stream of revenues and expenditures expected to be generated by the project. These revenue-expenditure forecasts are then presented to corporate management by the general manager. At the same time, revenue-expenditure forecasts are being submitted by the general managers of other business units for projects that they would like to have funded. The problem faced by corporate management is a *capital budgeting* problem. That is, a decision must be made as to which projects should be funded and at what level of support so as to achieve overall corporate goals and objectives.

Most companies utilize one of two alternative investment criteria to evaluate major investment projects: *net present value* and *internal rate of return.* An investment project can be viewed as a stream of positive or negative cash flows. Since these flows occur in the future over the life of the investment, we are interested in calculating their value at the beginning of the planning horizon, before the project is even actually initiated. The *net present value* (NPV) of an investment project is the value today of the project's future stream of net benefits (revenue minus costs).[1] Stated alternatively, the present value of an investment represents the amount the firm would be prepared to pay for a project with a particular stream of net cash flows associated with it. If NPV is positive, the project should be accepted because it will increase the market value of the firm. Conversely, if NPV is negative, the project would reduce the market value of the firm and the project should be rejected. (One disadvantage of this criterion is that it is necessary to assume a specific interest rate in order to calculate the NPV.)

An alternative to the NPV criterion is that of *internal rate of return* (IRR),[2] which usually yields the same result as the NPV but with one distinct advantage over NPV. The IRR does not require the specification of an interest rate for present-value computation. The IRR itself is defined to be that interest (or discount) rate that makes NPV zero. One interpretation of the IRR is that it is the value of the interest rate that would make the firm indifferent between undertaking and not undertaking a particular project. The IRR is useful in summarizing the economic merit of an investment project entirely on the basis of revenues and costs. Whether the project should or should not be undertaken then depends on the comparison of the IRR with the market interest rate or the cost of capital, which is the weighted average of the cost of debt and the cost of equity.

LIMITATIONS OF CAPITAL BUDGETING

Thus far our discussion has concentrated on single investment projects, that is, situations in which the parent company must decide whether to accept or reject a particular project. Furthermore, we have argued that the project should be accepted if NPV is positive or if the IRR is greater than the cost of capital. These decision rules are relatively straightforward and are described in most textbooks on managerial economics and capital budgeting. But now let us suppose that we have not one project to evaluate but several—projects from across the company's entire portfolio of businesses. Furthermore, let us suppose that many of these businesses have interdependent demand functions and production processes, which means, in turn, that the projects will have interdependent revenue forecasts and expenditure forecasts. Suppose too that corporate management wants to decide not only which projects to support but also wants to determine what level of investment to make in those projects. As a result of this additional information, the complexity of the managerial decision problem increases precipitously. Indeed, our capital budgeting problem is now so complex that it literally exceeds the state-of-the-art mathematical modeling techniques that are available for the solution of capital budgeting problems. Although analytical techniques exist in theory for solving problems of this type, in actual practice I know of no examples where this problem has been solved using formal analytical methods. But this is only one of the major limitations of modern capital budgeting techniques in dealing with investment decisions involving interdependent projects and business units. A second practical problem associated with capital budgeting techniques exists.

Up to now, we have treated the investment problem of corporate strategy as a problem of complete certainty; that is, we have assumed that for each investment alternative there is one and only one outcome. Or, to put it even more precisely, we have assumed that each investment alternative yields a specific NPV and a specific IRR. However, in the real world, there may be several possible revenue and cost streams associated with a given instrument project, each of which may produce different values of NPV and IRR for each project. In the absence of complete certainty, management no longer envisages a one-to-one relationship between alternative courses of action and outcomes. If management is able to estimate the probability that a given outcome will be associated with a particular investment alternative, then decision making is said to take place under conditions of *risk*. If management is unable to estimate the probabilities associated with different investment-outcome combinations, then we have decision making under *uncertainty*. *Risk analysis* refers to investment problems under risk and uncertainty.[3]

Although risk analysis is a popular topic in most graduate schools of business, it is seldom used by corporations as an analytical tool for evaluating investment decisions. There are several reasons that this is so. First of all, most of the capital budgeting techniques that involve risk analysis assume that managers already know the probability distributions of the revenue and cost streams associated with each project. In reality, such probability distributions are usually not known and are not easy to estimate empirically. Furthermore, many of the risk analysis tools used for capital budgeting involve computer simulation models. Such simulation experiments may require a large number of replications and, therefore, substantial blocks of computer time, which can be prohibitively expensive. In addition, simulation experiments are likely to generate a host of sophisticated statistical problems related to validation, experimental design, and data analysis. A final drawback is that formal risk analysis techniques are difficult to sell to senior executives. The number of corporate executives who are comfortable with probability distributions and statistical inference is very small, constituting a mere subset of senior executives.

In summary, although there are some very sophisticated capital budgeting tools available to management, they tend to be woefully inadequate when applied to highly interdependent investment projects under conditions of risk and uncertainty. To address investment problems of this type, we need an approach to strategic planning that can process large amounts of information pertaining to project interdependencies and risk and uncertainty. The multidimensional team approach of the strategy matrix appears uniquely suited for handling complex investment problems of the type typically confronted by multibusiness companies.

THE RESOURCE ALLOCATION MATRIX

The resource allocation version of the strategy matrix developed by Shell Oil, IBM, and Squibb evolved in direct response to some of the limitations of both portfolio models and capital budgeting techniques when it came to solving investment problems that involved interdependent businesses. Underlying the resource allocation matrix is the assumption that the firm controls a portfolio of interdependent businesses that all share many of the common resources we have noted before, that is, human resources, R & D, raw materials, and plant and equipment. Each resource is managed by a functional vice-president or resource manager, and each business is managed by a business manager. Both managers report to a general manager, or matrix manager, who stands outside of the matrix.

A business team, consisting of individuals from the various functional or resource departments, manages each business and prepares a five-year business plan that includes objectives, goals, strategies, resource requirements, and analysis. Long before the business plans are presented to the matrix manager and the resource managers, however, the business team leaders meet in order to sort out any conflicts that have arisen among the businesses. Sometimes these conflicts stem from the interdependence of the businesses and sometimes from the fact that the businesses are competing for common resources. The business plans are then submitted to the matrix manager and the resource managers for evaluation and eventual approval. All of the business managers are expected to be present at these planning sessions. Once the individual business plans have been approved, it is then possible to develop an integrated plan that reflects the contribution of each of the individual business plans.

The resource managers are responsible for deploying the company's assets in a manner that is consistent with the business plans. To achieve the goals and objectives of the businesses, resource budgets and operating plans must be formulated. The whole philosophy underlying the resource allocation matrix is that the resources are there to support the businesses rather than to cater to the whims of the resource managers. Ultimately, the resource managers implement the business plans, but the business managers coordinate this activity and ensure that business goals and objectives are achieved.

Through this series of interactions between the business teams and the resource managers, the company attempts to sort out the complex task of resource allocation in such a way so that resources are committed to those businesses offering the greatest promise in terms of realizing corporate goals and objectives. As we have noted in previous chapters, such a team approach can generate and process an enormous amount of information about the linkages that exist among the various interdependent businesses and projects. Thus, without the aid of sophisticated computer models and their inherent limitations, business teams and resource managers eventually converge on a solution to the company's resource allocation problem. To illustrate the application of the resource allocation strategy matrix, examples taken from Shell Oil, IBM, and Squibb will now be discussed.

The Shell Oil Resource Allocation Matrix

BACKGROUND

Although it ranked seventh in sales in 1984 among the American integrated oil companies, Shell consistently outperforms most of its major competitors with regard to return on investment. Between 1971 and 1981, it enjoyed the highest average return on investment of the top eight oil companies. Unlike its competitors, whose profits have been quite erratic, Shell's earnings per share increased steadily throughout the 1970s. In 1982, when Exxon, Mobil, and Texaco were all recording substantial decreases in net income, Shell's earnings fell only slightly. Finally, between 1980 and 1984, Shell reported the highest growth rate in earnings per share among the major American oil companies. In the eyes of many experts in the petroleum industry, Shell is viewed as the best managed company in the industry. Shell's management uses the strategy matrix to maintain this high level of financial performance.

My first contact with Shell Oil occurred in 1978, when I was brought in as a consultant and was asked to evaluate the strategic planning process the company had been using since 1972.[4] The planning process the management of Shell described to me turned out to be, in fact, the strategy matrix. Although at that time I was quite familiar with matrix management, I had never seen the concept used as a vehicle for organizing a company's strategic planning process. Several years later, long after my consultation with Shell Oil, I was given the opportunity to review the strategic planning processes of Velsicol Chemical and Federal Express. To my complete and utter amazement, I suddenly realized that the manner in which they were doing strategic planning was almost identical to what I had seen at Shell Oil in 1978. Furthermore, the reasons Velsicol Chemical and Federal Express cited for using the matrix management approach to strategic planning were exactly the same as those I had heard from Shell Oil several years earlier.

When Shell Oil introduced the strategy matrix in 1972, the entire international petroleum industry was attempting to find ways to survive when supplies of crude oil were in excess, crude oil prices were relatively low ($3 per barrel), and virtually no growth in corporate profits could be seen. Most international oil companies like Shell were vertically integrated, a structure that ensured them a higher degree of market control over the marketing of downstream products derived from crude oil and natural gas, both of which were available in abundant quantity and low price. Vertical integration was a strategy that attempted to increase the value added by manufacturing in the petroleum industry so as to extract a higher price for downstream petroleum-based products. Since the petrochemical business at that time was completely stagnant and did not appear to offer much in the way of growth potential, a strategy of vertical integration made a lot of sense.

Against this background of relatively unfavorable economic factors, Shell Oil faced another series of complications in producing and marketing petroleum products. One of these arose out of the way in which integrated oil companies are organized, most being decentralized either functionally or geographically. Functionally organized companies, such as Gulf Oil Corporation, typically are subdivided according to three major activities: exploration and production, refining and marketing, and chemicals. Other companies, such as Texaco, have moved to a decentralized approach along geographic lines. Texaco USA, for example, is a fully integrated oil company that carried out each of the above functions. While both Gulf and Texaco have considered the SBU approach, they have recognized that there is a very serious problem in attempting to apply traditional portfolio models to oil companies like themselves. Many oil companies that claim to be decentralized in fact are not decentralized regarding crude oil allocation to specific refineries and operating units. With rare exceptions, crude oil is allocated at the corporate level in most major oil companies. Individual operating companies are not free to buy and sell crude oil in response to changes in market conditions without approval from the corporate supply and distribution department.

The way in which integrated oil companies make their crude oil allocation decisions results in a situation where the decision becomes a twofold problem. Not only must a decision be made about the allocation of cash to individual refineries and operating units, but a decision must also be made about how to allocate crude oil. These complications make it virtually impossible for integrated oil companies to employ either the analytical portfolio models described in the previous chapter or the simplistic capital budgeting models just described. Further complicating life for integrated oil companies is the fact that most of the products that are produced in oil refineries and petrochemical processing plants ultimately derive from crude oil and natural gas. And these products—whether they be gasolines, lubricants, or agricultural chemical products—all flow through the same processes in the same refineries. It is virtually impossible to disentangle one product from another in terms of utilization of refinery and chemical plant capacity. Petrochemical products manufactured by petroleum companies are thus highly interdependent as to their utilization of shared resources. In addition, they often compete with one another in the marketplace! Thus, when Shell Oil introduced the strategy matrix into its Chemical Products division in 1972, the action represented an attempt to cope with a very unfavorable economic environment and a set of complex interdependencies throughout its entire product mix.

To meet the challenge associated with the interdependencies existing within the company, in 1972 Shell turned to the strategy matrix for its chemical products business, which, a year later, it consolidated with its oil products business into a single Products Business. At the same time, the company also implemented a full-blown resource allocation matrix across the entire Products Business. (*Oil Products* is the term Shell uses to describe its downstream operations, including refining and marketing.) Obviously, Shell's adoption of the matrix was given considerable impetus in 1973 when the price of crude oil shot up to nearly $30 a barrel in response to the pricing policies of the oil-producing countries in the Middle East. In the final analysis, Shell was looking for the flexibility to meet the challenge posed by both a hostile economic environment and by a highly interdependent product mix. There were no options available to Shell other than to turn to the strategy matrix.

THE SHELL OIL STRATEGY MATRIX

Shell produces over seventy different products spread over its Oil and Chemical Products divisions. Seven different refineries across the United States are operated by Shell to produce gasoline, jet fuel, and, increasingly, feedstocks for chemicals. These are the major products of the Oil Products business. The Chemical Products business is a major supplier of olefins, aromatics, detergent alcohols, thermoplastic rubber, epoxy resins, vinyl chloride monomers, agricultural herbicides, and insecticides, to mention only a few. Shell cites two basic objectives for Oil Products: first, to remain among the most efficient and profitable of the major petroleum companies, and, second, to position itself to perform well in periods of crude oil shortage, oversupply, or relative supply-demand balance. The basic strategy for Chemical Products is to invest selectively for continued cost efficiencies in all its major chemical product lines, and to expand capacity in those products and markets where Shell Chemical Company has especially strong positions. Exxon, Texaco, Mobil, and most of the other major petroleum companies manage oil prod-

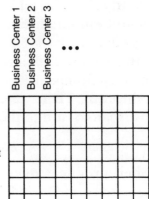

BUSINESS CENTERS

1. Capital
2. Refinery Capacity
3. Hydrocarbon Supplies
4. Research and Development
5. Human Reources
6. Marketing
7. Distribution System

STRATEGIC RESOURCES

Figure 4–1

The Shell Oil Company Resource Allocation Matrix

SOURCE: William W. Reynolds, Shell Oil Company

ucts and chemical products as two separate businesses. Shell consolidated them into a single business.

The version of Shell's strategy matrix we will turn to is the full products matrix that was in effect between 1974 and 1983. This product matrix has now evolved into a series of interconnected matrices. Although it is not possible to describe all of the various matrices of the company, we can indicate the nature of the evolutionary changes that have taken place with a universal products matrix. Figure 4–1 describes the products matrix as Shell Oil implemented it in the late 1970s. Note that the two dimensions of the matrix are *business centers* and *business resources*.

Business Centers. Prior to 1972, when the matrix

was introduced into Shell's Chemical Products business, there existed six completely autonomous divisions in the business, each possessing its own manufacturing goals, R & D, and financial functions, as well as its own support staff. When the matrix was first implemented, these divisions were reorganized as thirteen business centers. A "business center," according to Shell economics consultant William W. Reynolds, is simply a collection of products that are relatively homogeneous in nature. For example, polypropylene, catalysts, and agricultural chemicals are each treated as business centers at Shell. Business centers compete for a variety of strategic resources—capital, refining capacity, hydrocarbon supplies, research and development, and qualified people. The principal difference between a business center and an SBU is the fact that Shell assumes at the outset that a business center may generate products that will be sold in the same market and that will compete within the company for certain shared resources, such as crude oil and refinery capacity.

At Shell, each business center is overseen by its own manager, who reports to a business unit manager. A business unit is simply a self-contained business defined by area or product, and may contain one or more business centers. The unit managers report to a Products Division president—one for Refining and Marketing, and one for Chemical Products, both of whom report to an executive vice-president. Business unit managers work with resource managers to develop a set of strategic options, including research and development, operations and marketing, all of which require employing the company's scarce resources. The managers prepare for their businesses a ten-year strategic plan, which consists of goals, objectives, business strategies, and resource requirements. Performance of the business unit is judged by ROI, net income, and net cash flow against targets. Specific milestones are established to track performance and to signal when a change in strategic goals is needed. Business units compete thus with each other for allocations of the company's resources based on their performance and position in the portfolio.

Strategic Resources. Strategic resources in operations and engineering, on the other hand, are the responsibility of a vice-president of manufacturing who oversees quality of performance, career planning, and professional skill maintenance. The vice-president of manufacturing also reports to the executive vice-president, as do support staff managers for finance, employee relations, and planning. One individual is ultimately responsible for the allocation of the strategic resources across the portfolio of business units at Shell. The business units are encouraged to operate freely until one of the resource constraints becomes binding. The annual planning process brings into focus a balanced view between business unit needs and resource constraints. The executive vice-president and the vice-presidents, together with corporate management, make the final judgment on the course to be followed.

Central Management. As I indicated earlier, the executive vice-president presides over both arms of

Shell's strategy matrix. As the matrix manager, he stands outside the matrix and thus functions as the interface with the General Executive Office, made up of the CEO and the executive vice-presidents, which forms the central management team. The duties of central management at Shell, according to William W. Reynolds, are to manage the culture, lead change, set financial targets, allocate resources, define long-term business objectives, and define the role of the corporation in the surrounding society.

Decision Support Systems. Shell's application of the strategy matrix appears to be the most advanced application of this concept in existence today. Although the company's treatment of the portfolio problem of strategic planning is relatively informal, it uses computer-based decision support systems to arrive at the investment allocation decisions described above. Computer-based systems are used in making business strategy decisions as well. Specifically, Shell uses computer-based planning models to support the optimization of its refinery operations across the hydrocarbon-related portfolio of businesses. Each business center employs a decision support system known as IFPS to produce pro forma financial statements to be used in evaluating the effects of alternative business strategies. Simple financial models simulate the effects of various business strategies when different external environment scenarios are proposed. The information gleaned from these models lends support to the business unit managers' requests for strategic resources.

One benefit of Shell's application of the strategy

matrix is that the allocation of resources across business units is particularly noteworthy. Perhaps more important than the actual solution to the company's resource allocation problem itself is the ability of the strategy matrix to help senior management assign economic values to those strategic resources that are in short supply. Decisions to invest in additional strategic resources can thus be weighed against other portfolio options, such as acquisitions and new ventures. To illustrate this point, I suggest that if the strategy matrix did nothing except influence Shell to avoid buying a copper mine, then it has probably been worth its weight in gold. (Sohio, Indiana Standard, and Atlantic Richfield have all incurred substantial losses from recently acquired copper mines.)

EXPERIENCE

Shell's original use of the resource allocation matrix can be summarized as follows: First, business strategies are designed and executed in a highly decentralized manner by the managers of individual business units. Second, investment or resource allocation strategies across the portfolio of business centers are negotiated between the business unit managers and the strategic resource managers. A senior vice-president resolves conflicts between business unit managers and resource managers. Third, portfolio decisions concerned with which business centers will be supported and how they will be financed are made by senior corporate management. In the company's 1981 annual report, CEO John F. Bookout said the following about Shell's resource allocation matrix:

We manage Oil and Chemical Products as an integrated organization in order to utilize the Company's resources most efficiently. Integration gives us flexibility to direct hydrocarbon products with the best relative returns and strongest market demand. . . . Long term, we can focus our people, research programs, and capital investments where they are expected to generate the highest profits; strong growth businesses—whether in Oil Products or Chemical Products—get the most support.

Matrix management remains highly important at Shell Oil today. The corporate culture of the company clearly reflects the effects of a dozen years of team building. However, there is no longer a single matrix at Shell; rather, a series of federated matrices have been created. For example, the Products division was recently split again into two divisions—a Chemical division and a Refining and Marketing (R & M) division. The Chemical division is now composed of four business units, including polymers and catalysts, detergents, solvents, and agricultural products. Thus, the Chemical division remains a modified matrix with eight business centers. Refining and Marketing has also evolved into two product-oriented business units, including lubricants and three business centers. These recent changes reflect the fact that the original Products matrix for both Chemical and Oil Products divisions represented overconsolidation. The new, less consolidated federated matrices at Shell are more flexible and more effectively balance power between business center managers and resource managers.

In reviewing Shell Oil's experience with the strategy matrix since 1972, an obvious question comes to mind: What alternatives to the strategy matrix might the company have considered? The answer is that there really were no other alternatives available. The combination of a very volatile economic environment and a highly interdependent product mix posed a challenge that other planning models could not adequately meet. As pointed out, traditional divisional planning of the type used for many years by General Motors, General Electric, and other divisionalized corporations could not even begin to cope with Shell's cobweb of interdependencies. Shell Oil is a very big company. It needed a planning process flexible enough to respond to a rapidly changing environment, and the matrix offered it. Not only were analytical portfolio models and traditional capital budgeting techniques inadequate to respond to the production and marketing interdependencies that prevailed throughout Shell Oil's product mix, they also did not provide the right kind of information for making these complex resource allocation decisions. The participatory, team approach used by Shell provided more information, and in a more timely fashion, than could be provided by the myopic portfolio models and capital budgeting techniques.

IBM

With annual sales in excess of $50 billion and operations in 125 countries throughout the world, IBM is the second largest company after General Motors, using the strategy matrix. IBM's operations, with minor exceptions, are in information-handling systems, that is, supplying equipment and services for solving the increasingly complex problems of business, government, science, space exploration, defense, education, medicine, and numerous other areas of human endeavor. IBM's products include data processing machines and systems, telecommunications systems and products, information distributors, office systems, typewriters, copiers, educational and testing materials, and related supplies and services. Most products are both leased and sold throughout IBM's worldwide marketing organizations. Selected products are distributed through authorized dealers and re-marketers.

Although IBM has made extensive use of matrix management since 1959, it did not begin using the strategy matrix for its strategic planning process until 1972, the same year, coincidentally, in which the strategy matrix was introduced independently at Shell Oil.[5] Three facts influenced IBM's decision to introduce the strategy matrix. First, there was the sheer size of the company. Whether measured in total sales, number of different products, or scope of its international operations, IBM is a giant. Because of its size, the company found it increasingly difficult to manage such a diverse yet highly interdependent product line. Even someone with little knowledge of the office equipment and data processing industry can easily recognize the production and marketing interdependencies that characterize the industry. Second, IBM was beginning to face intense competition from abroad, particularly from Japan and West Germany. The company wisely perceived that it had a definite need for increased flexibility if it wished to respond successfully in a highly competitive international environment. Third, as we have previously indicated, IBM's decision to introduce the matrix was a response to the intense legal pressures brought upon the company as a result of the lawsuit by the U.S. Justice Department. The company, indeed, was forced to operate under the watchful eye of the government throughout the decade of the 1970s.

By the early 1970s, a divisional approach to strategic planning was out of the question for IBM. The company produced too many interdependent products in too many different divisions for sale in too many geographic locations for a divisional approach to be viable. Furthermore, IBM had never made use of any of the so-called portfolio models described in chapter 3. It was obvious to everyone at IBM that these simplistic two-dimensional diagrams did not possess the power or flexibility to respond to the complex needs of a company like IBM. With nearly fifteen years of experience in the use of the strategy matrix, IBM's commitment today to matrix-oriented strategic planning is virtually without equal in the United States.

According to IBM Planning Systems Director Abraham Katz, "Just about every company must be concerned with products and geography. Many organize in terms of one or the other dimension—by product or by geographic area. But when the organization gets large enough, dynamic enough, and complex enough, we have to recognize the multidimensional nature of the problem of planning and manage as a matrix."

The two dimensions underlying IBM's adaptation of the resource allocation matrix are *profit centers* and *business areas*, which are analogous, respectively, to Shell Oil's strategic resources and business centers. Not unlike Shell, IBM does not rely on a single strategy matrix but rather makes use of a variety of matrices throughout the entire company. For expository purposes, however, we shall restrict ourselves to the overall corporate strategy matrix represented by figure 4-2.

PROFIT CENTERS

Basically, IBM is organized into five major profit centers, as is indicated by figure 4-2. The Information Systems and Technology Group (ISTG) has worldwide development and U.S. manufacturing responsibility for three product systems. The ISTG produces large, complex systems, which include central processors; storage systems, which include tape units, disk products, and mass storage systems; and logic, memory, and special semiconductor devices. The Information Systems and Communications Group (ISCG), on the other hand, takes worldwide development and U.S. manufacturing responsibility for telecommunications systems, office systems, display products, and distribution industry systems. This group also manufactures typewriters, copiers, and systems for banking and manufacturing indus-

IBM

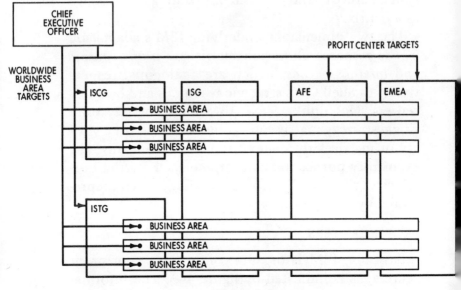

Figure 4–2

IBM Strategy Matrix: Profit Centers and Business Areas

SOURCE: Abraham Katz, IBM Corporation

tries and for peripheral equipment, including printers, copier systems, keyboards, diskettes, and associated supplies. The ISCG also oversees the development of small and intermediate-sized general purpose systems, and robotic systems.

The Information Systems Group (ISG) is part of the ISTG and ISCG profit centers. This group provides maintenance and related support services within the United States and its territories for systems and products developed by ISCG and ISTG. It has marketing and field administration responsibility within the United States and its territories for the full standard line of IBM products. ISG also formulates worldwide business strategy for information processing supplies and accessories as well as for manufacturing or procurement, and marketing within the United States and its territories of IBM supplies and services.

In addition to ISTG, ISCG, and ISG, the company operates two other profit centers: IBM World Trade Europe/Middle East/Africa and IBM World Trade Americas/Far East. Each of these organizations assumes regional responsibility for manufacturing, marketing, and servicing IBM's complete product line in its respective geographic area. Through its subsidiary, IBM Europe, which is headquartered in Paris, IBM Europe/Middle East/Africa controls the company's operations in over eighty countries. The territory covered by IBM Americas/Far East extends across four continents. This profit center handles IBM operations in the remaining countries, including Australia, Brazil, Canada, and Japan. There are also a number of corporate staff functions and special activities within IBM that are not shown in figure 4–2. The corporation is vertically integrated and produces approximately 50 percent of the electronic components it uses in its forty plants, which are scattered throughout the world. Profit center managers are appointed by the CEO and are assigned five-year financial targets, which always include net earnings before taxes and return on controllable assets. Profit centers focus primarily on productivity and profitability.

BUSINESS AREAS

Business areas form the second dimension of IBM's resource allocation matrix. Business areas are analogous to SBUs, but are acknowledged from the outset by IBM to be completely interdependent with regard to manufacturing, development, marketing, and service. Among the ten business areas are processors, terminals, storage, telecommunications, typewriters, application software, and copiers. Business area managers concern themselves with strategies aimed at revenue growth. These managers also are appointed by the CEO and see themselves as entrepreneurs who work with a team of people representing the five profit centers.

STRATEGIC PLANNING PROCESS

The objectives for IBM's strategic planning process were succinctly outlined in the company's 1982 annual report:

1 *Profitable Growth.* We are firmly committed to profitable growth. We are expanding our traditional business and investing in a variety of new entrepreneurial opportunities with high, long-term potential.
2 *Product Leadership.* We intend to be the product leaders, to stay in the forefront of the industry in technology, reliability, quality and value across our entire product line.
3 *Low-Cost Producer.* We are concentrating on efficiency in every aspect of our work. We want to be not only the low-cost producer of the highest quality products in the industry, but also the low-cost developer, seller, and servicer.

Abraham Katz refers to IBM's strategic planning system as the "central nervous system of IBM." If it appears somewhat complex, it is because it is one of the most sophisticated planning systems in existence anywhere in the world today. There is absolutely nothing simple about IBM's planning process, but it works, and it works very well.

As we summarize the planning process used by IBM in the following paragraphs, one other thought should be kept in mind. IBM does not distinguish between strategies and tactics. According to Katz, what IBM possesses is a set of "nested strategies." Again, it is interesting to note the similarity of this concept to Shell Oil's "federated matrices." IBM's matrix-oriented strategic planning process involves two interdependent cycles. A business investment cycle begins in the spring and focuses on strategic direction and investment. A commitment plan (operating plan) and long-range outlook cycle kicks off in autumn. This second cycle focuses on operating commitments and reaffirms longer-term forecasts.[6]

The planning cycle begins with the CEO's assignment of strategic targets to the business area and profit center managers. Operating unit managers then develop goals for their units that will enable them to reach the fifth-year targets. Operating units are subdivisions of business areas and profit centers. Managers of branch offices and of laboratories are examples of operating unit managers. Depending on the nature of the operating unit, these goals, year by year, include such things as expense-to-revenue ratios, marketing goals, and productivity ratios.

Given targets and goals, the plan is then developed in view of the product and environmental assumptions made by the operating units. The Corporate Economics staff provides valuable input at this stage as well. Using the product and economic assumptions, the operating unit produces an overall set of business volumes, which are then translated into workloads, resources, and cost/expense ratios. Computer-based planning models are widely used in the process. The overall requirements are then integrated into a balanced business plan, which is one that considers both growth and profitability. The autumn planning process proceeds in a similar fashion but results in the formulation of detailed operating plans and budgets.

Finally, IBM also employs "independent business units" for exploring suitable areas for diversification. Independent business units are very small businesses typically oriented around a single new product. They are operated as separate companies, having their own independent board of directors. IBM provides limited resources to evaluate new product ideas and to bring these products to the market. In 1984, there were fifteen independent business units within IBM, eleven of which operated within the United States. They include such diverse businesses as academic information systems and biomedical systems, financial services, graphics systems, industrial automation, and telecommunications carrier products. Across the ocean, European independent business units are providing products and services that are tailored to the needs of individual countries. Products are being provided in such fields as telecommunications, manufacturing, academic information systems, and information networks. In addition, independent business units in Japan are responsible for developing and introducing products that meet the unique needs of the Japanese marketplace.

In assessing the results of IBM's matrix-oriented, long-term strategic planning process, John R. Opel, IBM's chairman, expressed the views of the company's senior management in the company's 1983 annual report as follows:

The groundwork for our positive results the past two years was established back in the mid-1970s when, with a program of sizable investments in plant, equipment, research and development, we began to prepare for the great opportunities we saw ahead. Since then, we have reshaped our organization as necessary to adapt to a changing environment marked by the significant growth of our industry. Our strategy has focused on ensuring our full participation in that growth.

Central to IBM's strategy are four key business goals—growth, product leadership, efficiency, and profitability. To attain these goals in today's highly competitive environment, we have placed increased emphasis on innovative programs in the design, manufacture, and distribution of our products and services. These programs have started to produce results. We are moving higher volumes of products through our organization and into our customers' offices, at the same time maintaining effective cost control and high quality.

Squibb Pharmaceutical Products

E. R. Squibb and Sons is divided into four operating groups—pharmaceutical products, medical products, personal products, and corporate research and development. In 1981, the Squibb Pharmaceutical Products Group began using the strategy matrix for its U.S.-based operations. The evolution of Squibb's organizational structure and its strategic planning process closely parallels that of Dow-Corning. Squibb originally was organized along the traditional functional lines of marketing, finance, manufacturing, quality control, and human resources. However, in response to intense competitive pressures in the late 1970s, the company introduced a number of major new products, and this put enormous stress on its rigid, hierarchical organization structure. During this same time, the U.S. government became a much more influential force in the entire pharmaceutical industry, thus adding to the organizational stress of the Squibb Pharmaceutical Products Group.[7]

Not only did the Food and Drug Administration make it more difficult to obtain approval for the marketing and distribution of new pharmaceutical products, but by the late 1970s and early 1980s, the industry felt considerable pressure to help contain the cost of medical care. The pressure for cost reduction has accelerated in recent years as a result of the enactment of Medicare's prospective payment system, the so-called DRG (Diagnostic Related Group) legislation. Increased urgings for improved cost effectiveness and calls for reduced prices made it painfully apparent that a new approach was needed for planning and monitoring Squibb's complex array of pharmaceutical products. A functional organization structure and a traditional hierarchical planning process increasingly proved to be inadequate to meet the needs of a company that operated thirty-three manufacturing facilities and was attempting to compete in more than fifty countries.

Richard A. Druckman, vice-president of Strategic Planning and Management Information Systems, at Squibb, clarified for me the rationale underlying his company's introduction of the strategy matrix: "The purpose of the strategy matrix at Squibb was to replace our traditional hierarchical approach to management with a strategic management system which would provide top management with a stronger sense of direction in responding to resource allocation problems in an increasingly complex world." As with Florida Power, SCE&G, and Velsicol Chemical, the introduction of the strategy matrix at Squibb was steered through the storm by a new CEO and a corporatewide reorganization. Indeed, without unflinching commitment on the part of the new helmsman, it would have been impossible to change the culture of Squibb. CEO Jan Leschly expressed his feelings about the changes he perceives in the corporate culture at Squibb Pharmaceutical Products Group. "Our management should adopt a management style which is consistent with the needs of employees. Accordingly, we believe that an appropriate style for us must be participatory. It must promote trust and confidence, and it must result in employee satisfaction." It is precisely these values around which the strategy matrix at Squibb is today based.

As a result of the increased product orientation of the company, the Squibb Pharmaceutical Group was reorganized in 1982 into four basic business groups —ethical, consumer, animal health, and diagnostics. Each of these groups was in turn subdivided into business areas, of which there are a total of fifteen. Each business area is managed by a business team consisting of people who are recruited from across the company's seven shared resources. Thus, Squibb's strategy matrix is based on two dimensions—seven resources and fifteen businesses. The implementation of the strategy matrix at Squibb closely parallels the process used by Shell Oil. However, more than 150 people participate in the company's strategic planning process. Squibb's senior management makes a special effort to link the company's operating plans to the strategic plans of the business areas. Although the operating plans are controlled by the resource managers, they are driven by the business area strategic plans. The strategic planning process and the budget are inextricably linked. Basically, year one of the strategic plan is the budget for the following year, which is, of course, exactly as it should be. Squibb also makes use of portfolio models and business simulation models to evaluate strategic plans at the business area level.

Although the principal strategy matrix used by Squibb contains the elements of what we have called the resource allocation matrix, in reality, the Squibb Pharmaceutical Group makes use of a series of interconnected matrices, the dimensions of which include business groups, resources, issues, and regional centers. As previously noted, the Squibb Pharmaceutical Group also operates within a portfolio strategy matrix that consists of three corporatewide strategies cutting across the ethical, consumer, animal health, and diagnostics businesses. Squibb's third strategy matrix is a geographic resource allocation matrix in which the dimensions cover five geographic regions in the United States as well as critical resources.

The increased flexibility provided by the strategy matrix has enabled Squibb to respond vigorously to competitive forces in the marketplace. The introduction of generic drugs and the fact that some of its patents have recently expired were prime motivators for introducing the matrix at Squibb. But the major benefit of the strategy matrix, according to Druckman, is that "it promotes teamwork and is conducive to a participatory style of management which encourages people to work together."

Another difference between the strategy matrix and the planning process Squibb previously used is that senior management now has access to substantially more information on which to make critical decisions. The participatory nature of the matrix encourages a broad exchange of views among managers as to the best solution to a particular problem. The matrix was not implemented overnight; rather, it evolved over several years. As the corporate culture gradually began to change, more and more managers embraced the shared values underlying the approach. In fact, by 1984, there was such a broad-based consensus among the senior managers at Squibb that they were able to formalize a set of seven shared values for the entire Pharmaceutical Group. These included excellence, return on investment, high-quality products, creativity and innovation, participatory management, teamwork, and risk taking.

During the first four years in which Squibb used the strategy matrix as the basis for its strategic planning, pretax profits for the Squibb Pharmaceutical Group increased at a compound growth rate of 35 percent per year. With these encouraging results, it is not surprising that the company is beginning to extend the use of the strategy matrix to its international operations. Already it had introduced the matrix into West Germany and the United Kingdom. Finally, in assessing Squibb's experience with the matrix, Druckman believes that three elements have been particularly important to the successful application of the matrix at Squibb. Druckman cites the wholehearted commitment of the CEO as the number one element influencing the success of the matrix, with multidisciplinary planning teams, and attention to detail following not far behind in importance.

Conclusions

I firmly believe that the principal reason that Shell Oil, IBM, and Squibb, among many others, have turned to the resource allocation strategy matrix is that this approach to planning overcomes some of the limitations of portfolio models and capital budgeting techniques in determining what level of resource commitment to make to interdependent businesses. The multidimensional team approach of the resource allocation matrix cuts right through to the heart of the interdependence issue and attempts to process the information that is needed to make such complex resource allocation decisions. Rather than relying on simplistic portfolio models, sophisticated capital budgeting models, or mechanistic computer-based planning models, the resource allocation matrix draws upon the combined judgment of business teams and resource managers for sorting out the problems of project interdependence and risk and uncertainty. By drawing on multiple sources of information from across the portfolio of businesses and the entire set of shared resources, resource allocation decisions rely on a variety of viewpoints.

I am not necessarily suggesting that standard capital budgeting techniques such as net present value and internal rate of return should be thrown to the wind and abandoned forever. Rather, it is my feeling that these myopic techniques, when taken by themselves, do not generate enough information on which to make major resource allocation decisions for highly interdependent businesses such as those found in the three companies we have just reviewed. Indeed, most companies that use the strategy matrix also employ capital budgeting techniques. The resource allocation strategy matrix is not a substitute for capital budgeting techniques. Rather, it extends the capability of capital budgeting so that it can address more complex problems when interdependent businesses are involved.

In summary, the resource allocation matrix uses participatory management to provide increased flexibility in dealing with the information requirements of interdependent projects that cut across interdependent businesses. By broadening the scope of managerial participation in major resource allocation decisions, it becomes less important to depend on myopic quantitative techniques when making decisions. Ultimately, the matrix is used to draw on the creative powers of human beings to replace a set of rigid, naive analytical tools that have proven to be inadequate for the job for which they were originally intended.

5 _____

BUSINESS STRATEGY: HOW SHOULD EACH BUSINESS COMPETE?

_____

The Problem of Business Strategy

IN the two previous chapters, the strategy matrix was applied across the entire portfolio of businesses owned by a single corporation. Chapter 3 was concerned with a set of top-down, corporatewide portfolio strategies, while chapter 4 addressed the problem of determining what level of resources to commit to the different businesses in the portfolio. The focus of this chapter will be on the application of the strategy matrix to a single business, one that may either be a stand-alone business or one unit of a set of businesses in a company's portfolio.

The problem of *business strategy* involves positioning the business in the marketplace and selecting the appropriate marketing, production, and organizational activities that will enable the business to compete effectively in the marketplace. That is, the challenge facing the business is to achieve its goals and objectives in light of given assumptions about the external environment. Although the literature on strategic planning abounds with books and articles on portfolio planning, capital budgeting, and the like, the strategic planning process within a specific business unit typically receives short shrift. Perhaps the reason that this is so is that the fantasy of the CEO ensconced in corporate headquarters while managing a large portfolio of businesses located in faraway places holds much more glamour than the image of the executive in shirt sleeves who is embroiled in the nitty-gritty detail of planning for a single business. Alternatively, perhaps some people assume that strategic planning within a single-business unit is so simple that it does not merit serious attention. For whatever reason strategic planning at the business unit level has been ignored, it is a serious omission, one that has led to some extremely ineffective ways of doing strategic planning.

As indicated before, the vast majority of individual business units in this country are organized along functional lines. In those business units that utilize formal strategic planning, it is quite usual for them to attempt to organize strategic planning along the same lines. Each functional manager or officer prepares a strategic plan that includes goals, objectives, and strategies. For example, the vice-president of finance may desire a specific return on investment target for next year to be achieved using a strategy of very conservative cash management. Such a financial plan makes absolutely no sense, however, without first considering the competitive environment, the availability and price of key raw materials, and the attitude of the company's blue-collar workers toward management. Indeed, one could argue that the whole concept of independent functional strategic plans is not only absurd but in most cases is actually impossible as well.

What I am proposing here is that the functions of finance, marketing, production, human resources development, and R & D are completely interdependent activities. For example, the implementation of a production plan depends on the availability of cash to finance inventories and on the existence of customers who will purchase the products. Functional strategic plans cannot be formulated in a vacuum. Furthermore, if plans should happen to be developed independently of each other, any attempt to integrate them into a coherent strategic plan for the entire business is likely to become bogged down in cumbersome detail. In fact, the attempt may be well-nigh impossible.

The principal idea underlying the strategy matrix at the business unit level is that strategic planning should be viewed as an activity in which goals, objectives, and strategies are integrated across the entire business. With the strategy matrix, managers are asked to think in terms of business goals and strategies rather than in terms of functional goals and strategies. Under the strategy matrix, it is business plans, not functional plans, that drive the business. Furthermore, from the outset, it is assumed that these business plans cut across the company's functional lines. To illustrate the principles associated with this business strategy matrix, I will now give a detailed account of Velsicol Chemical Corporation's experience with the matrix. This will be followed by brief illustrations taken from the experiences of Federal Express and Florida Power.

Velsicol Chemical: A Case Study

Velsicol Chemical is one of the four operating companies of Northwest Industries that uses the strategy matrix for business planning. The strategy matrix was introduced at Velsicol in 1979 after a completely new management team came on board, which it did following a series of well-publicized and major environmental problems. With annual sales of a little over $200 million, Velsicol is one of the smallest firms successfully to implement the strategy matrix. Velsicol has achieved a remarkable corporate turnaround since Northwest Industries CEO Ben W. Heineman sent William Howard Beasley, III, to the troubled company in 1978. At that time, Velsicol faced what appeared to be an endless stream of environmental and legal problems arising from its production of two flame retardants, PBB and Tris, and the pesticide

Phosvel. Beasley's mandate from Heineman was straightforward: "Go to Velsicol and clean it up. Do whatever is necessary to do so, spend whatever money is necessary to do so, just don't gold-plate it." Four years later, in early 1982, Heineman had this to say about Velsicol: "With most of its earlier problems either disposed of or largely provided for, Velsicol has just had the best quarter of any in its history."

Velsicol Chemical specializes in the manufacture and sale of agricultural, pest control, and specialty chemicals. The agricultural chemicals produced by Velsicol fall primarily into the category of crop protection chemicals, principally herbicides. The majority of the company's pest control chemicals are insecticides, principally termiticides. Specialty chemicals include many of the intermediate chemicals that are required in the production of agricultural chemicals, as well as benzoic acid and its derivatives for use in plasticizers and other chemicals. Agricultural and pest control chemicals dominate Velsicol's production and sales activities.

Chemical products appear under various brand names and are sold to the agricultural, pest control, and industrial markets along a variety of routes—via distributors, dealers, manufacturing companies, and foreign governments. The company's principal products, however, are sold under the Banvel brand name. Velsicol operates four manufacturing plants in the United States as well as plants in Mexico and Brazil. Chemical products are sold in a highly competitive market, where competitors range in size from large, highly diversified companies to small specialty producers. Velsicol itself ranks as a major producer of certain herbicides and insecticides and benzoic acid derivatives.

When Howard Beasley introduced the strategy matrix at Velsicol, the company was not only facing major environmental problems arising from certain toxic chemicals it had produced, but it was also facing intense competition within an industry then suffering from an acute case of overcapacity. From the very outset, Beasley decided against reorganizing the company, his feeling being that Velsicol had gone through trauma enough. Given the multitude of legal and environmental problems the company had recently had to contend with, Beasley saw no advantage to introducing a radical change in organization structure. Also influencing his decision was the fact that many of the senior managers were new to their positions, having been recently brought in to replace the management team that had been there before Beasley took control of the company. For better or for worse, Beasley opted not to tinker with the functional organization structure already in place when he assumed command. Indeed, he was adamant in his objections to the suggestion that Velsicol consider adopting a matrix organization similar to the one employed by Dow-Corning.

While it was one thing to retain Velsicol's functional organization structure, it was quite another thing to try to respond to the company's plethora of environmental and competitive problems. A typical, straightforward functional approach to formulating and implementing strategies for solving these problems had little chance of being successful. The solutions to most of the company's problems typically involved support from several different functional areas. Given Velsicol's existing structure and functional planning process, who within the company would be expected to assume responsibility for formulating specific strategies and for coordinating the implementation of these strategies across functional lines? Obviously, as Beasley realized, something would have to give. Either the organization structure had to be changed or the strategic planning process would have to be altered. With assistance from an outside consultant, Beasley chose to redesign the company's strategic planning process, which resulted in Velsicol's adoption of the strategy matrix.

The consultant suggested that Velsicol segment itself into three businesses. Agricultural chemicals would make up one of these and specialty chemicals another. A third business would be established whose exclusive purpose would be the resolution of the company's past environmental and legal problems.

In this case study of Velsicol, we shall focus exclusively on the agricultural chemical business since it accounts for over 90 percent of the company's business. That is, we will treat Velsicol as a single-business company.

The second recommendation made by Beasley's outside consultant was that he should manage his agricultural chemical business by implementing fifteen different strategies—strategies that would cut across the functional lines of the company. Thus, a new strategic dimension was superimposed over the company's functional departments. According to Strategic Planning director David Barrington, "The strategies represent paths of resource commitment. Each strategy has certain costs and risks associated with it and will yield certain results, both in terms of financial performance and competitive position."

BUSINESS STRATEGIES

Business strategies at Velsicol Chemical and at other companies that use the business strategy matrix are usually either functionally oriented, market oriented, or are oriented around a product's life cycle. Functional strategies can include marketing, organizational development, and production operations but typically do not include finance at the business unit level. As we have previously noted, financial strategies are usually of relatively little importance to individual businesses or to operating companies that belong to conglomerates such as Northwest Industries. In the case of Velsicol Chemical, Northwest Industries acts as the company's banker.

Many of Velsicol's strategies can be identified as essentially marketing strategies. In a typical marketing strategy, there exist such elements as market identification, brand identification, channel selection, price, and advertising. That is, a marketing strategy is a composite of the aforementioned activities. In Michael E. Porter's book, *Competitive Strategy*, three widely used marketing strategies are described: cost leadership, product differentiation, and market focus.[1]

The *cost leadership* strategy derives its importance,

in part, from the popularity of The Boston Consulting Group's concept of the experience curve, which we described in chapter 3. Recall that according to experience curve theory, accumulated output leads to lower costs. Lower costs enable the firm to drop the price and thus increase its market share, which in turn leads to further increases in output, lower costs, and so on. According to Porter, "Cost leadership requires aggressive construction of efficient-scale facilities, vigorous pursuit of cost reductions from experience, tight cost and overhead control, avoidance of marginal customer accounts, and cost minimization in areas like R & D, service, sales force, advertising, and so on."[2] Among those firms noted for the successful application of the cost leadership strategy are Emerson Electric, Texas Instruments, and Black and Decker.

The main thrust of the *product differentiation* strategy is the attempt to influence buyers to perceive a particular product or service as unique. This is usually achieved through such means as advertising and promotion, technology, customer service, and dealer networks.[3] Toothpastes, household appliances, over-the-counter pharmaceutical products, and microcomputers are among the products that lend themselves to this approach to business strategy. Firms that have successfully applied differentiation as a competitive strategy are usually characterized by strong marketing skills, a high degree of creativity, sophisticated research and development, and first-rate product engineering. Velsicol has been particularly successful in differentiating its Banvel line of agricultural chemicals from those of its competitors. In the 1984 annual report of Northwest Industries, CEO Ben Heineman said, "The earnings of Velsicol Chemical Corporation remained strong in 1984 as the result of record demand for the Company's Banvel brand agricultural chemicals." Not only were Velsicol's earnings strong in 1984, but the company's sales and earnings both reached record highs during that year.

The *market focus* strategy identifies the particular consumer groups to whom the firm wants to sell its products and to whom it will then concentrate its marketing efforts. In contrast to the shotgun approach of cost leadership and product differentiation strategies, the market focus strategy is based on serving a specific target market very well, and so each functional policy is implemented with this thought in mind.[4]

Velsicol employs various combinations of the marketing strategies summarized above. With some products, the company competes by being the low cost producer. In other markets, product differentiation is the most effective strategy. However, the common denominator underlying all of Velsicol's strategies is agriculture. As a result of its adoption of the strategy matrix, Velsicol divested itself in 1981 of its principal industrial chemical operation, which had produced bromine and flame retardants. "We consider that we are the only worldwide chemical company that is now totally dedicated to agriculture," Howard Beasley told us not long ago. As other chemical companies continue to diversify their product mix, Velsicol followed a different path; it specialized in agriculture. To achieve this specialization, Velsicol has pursued a strategy of increased research and development and has also established a task force of agricultural specialists. The members of the task force are scattered around the world and are assigned the job of acquiring new products and technologies for the agricultural business.

In addition to functional strategies and market-oriented strategies, Velsicol also makes some use of product life-cycle strategies, which are similar to those mentioned in chapter 3 in conjunction with Arthur D. Little's equivalent of the growth-share matrix. That this perspective on business strategy has also been introduced at Velsicol is hardly surprising since the consultant who designed Velsicol's planning system originally came from Arthur D. Little. With the product life-cycle approach to business strategy, how effectively a business competes depends on where it is in its life cycle, whether it's an emerging, mature, or declining industry. *Emerging industries* are newly created industries that have arisen from modern technologies and the resulting new consumer needs. *Mature industries* are those in which the rate of growth has leveled off and competition for market share has increased among the firms in the industry. Finally, in *declining industries*, unit sales have actually experienced an absolute decline over time and are characterized by shrinking profit margins, reduced product lines, falling R & D and advertising expenditures, and a dwindling number of competitors.[5] At this point in time, the agricultural chemical industry is, at best, a mature industry and possibly even a declining industry. Given the relative maturity of the agricultural chemical industry, Velsicol has used a variety of strategies, depending on the particular product-market situation. For example, in some markets Velsicol has taken a strong *leadership* position in terms of market share. In other markets, it has created a *niche* for itself by defending a strong position in a particular market segment. It has either *harvested* (controlled disinvestment) or *divested* itself of its nonagricultural chemical businesses.

PLANNING PROCESS

Strategic planning at Velsicol begins each May with an off-site meeting at the company's research facilities near Chicago. The meeting is attended by the strategy managers, all of the strategic resource vice-presidents, and the CEO. Obviously, this meeting is not the initial contact between the strategy managers and the resource managers. The purpose of the off-site meeting is to set the stage for future, more intense, meetings between these two groups. More important, this informal meeting, according to former Velsicol CEO Beasley, "facilitates communications among managers, and raises their level of awareness of the interdependence of the different strategies." These sessions also encourage cooperation among strategy managers and between strategy managers and resource managers. The entire approach provides both strategy managers and resource managers with more of a sense of corporate direction than do traditional functional organization structures.

Each strategy manager prepares a strategic plan that consists of the following seven steps that are intended to be carried out roughly in the order given: (1) determination of competitive position, (2) strategy selection, (3) determination of resource requirements, (4) prediction of performance, (5) balancing of resource requirements against resource availability, (6) adoption of a final plan, and (7) setting of operating goals. Steps one through four of this process are presented at the off-site meeting. The remaining three are sorted out between the strategy managers and the resource managers over the course of the next two or three weeks before a final plan is approved by the senior management of Velsicol. Before the planning process actually begins, every Velsicol strategy manager is expected to review the multiscenario forecast of the external environment that has been produced by the corporate planning department of the parent company, Northwest Industries. This expectation ensures that every strategy manager comes to the planning meeting possessing assumptions about the external environment that are common to all participants.

COMPETITIVE ANALYSIS

Most of Velsicol's fifteen strategies are characterized by a strong product or market orientation. For this reason, strategy managers are instructed to prepare a competitive analysis for their particular strategies. Not unlike managers in many other companies, Velsicol's strategy managers have found Michael E. Porter's paradigm for analyzing the competitive environment particularly useful.[6] Porter defines five major forces that drive competition: first, the threat of potential new entrants into the market; second, the threat of substitution of existing products and services; third, the bargaining power of customers; fourth, the bargaining power of vendors; and, fifth, rivalry among existing competitors. Basically, a competitive analysis represents an attempt on the part of a strategy manager to construct a best-guess assessment of a particular competitor's strategic plan. That is, the strategy manager imagines himself in the shoes of his competitor and thus views the marketplace through the competitor's eyes. Once in this frame of mind, the strategy manager asks many questions. For instance: How does the competition perceive itself? What assumptions is it making about itself, the industry, and the economy? Obviously, such an analysis is hard to formulate since it may be very difficult to obtain reliable competitive data. And it is always difficult to view one's competitors objectively.

GOALS AND OBJECTIVES

Businesswide goals and objectives are formulated by the senior management of Velsicol before strategies are assigned to particular strategy managers. Even so, strategy managers are expected to review the business goals and objectives that will be affected by their respective strategies. When the strategy managers report back to the senior executives, they are given the opportunity to comment on the feasibility of achieving specific targets. If a strategy manager feels that a particular goal is unattainable, an appeal can always be made to the CEO of Velsicol for additional resources or for more time in which to reach the goal.

RESOURCE REQUIREMENTS

A business plan can be viewed as presenting the case to corporate management that specific resources should be allocated to one business rather than to another business. The strategic plan essentially serves as a rationalization of the resource requests of a particular business. The total resource requirements of Velsicol are in fact the sum of the resource requirements associated with the set of fifteen strategies. One of the primary responsibilities of each Velsicol strategy manager is to determine the resources required to implement the assigned strategy. Since strategy managers may not control the resources they need for implementing their strategies, they must negotiate for these resources with the functional resource managers. Optimally, resources will be allocated in accordance with the priorities assigned to the various strategies. In the event of unresolvable conflicts between resource managers and strategy managers, the matrix manager intervenes. In the case of Velsicol, this is the CEO.

ANALYSIS

Strategy managers of Velsicol supervise the analysis of their strategies. The analysis of business strategies evaluates the effects of alternative strategies on the business's goals and objectives. Certain firms that use the strategy matrix, such as Federal Express and

Florida Power, find it useful to develop computer-based planning models to evaluate the effects on financial performance of alternative business strategies. Velsicol, however, does not do so. And, unlike Shell Oil, Velsicol does allocate fixed, as well as variable, costs by strategy. It does this with a zero-based approach in that the majority of the fixed costs are allocated to the strategies that aim to maintain (but not improve) basic product-market positions. The contribution to net profit is the criterion used by the strategy managers to allocate resources to specific strategies. The final plans developed by the strategy managers evolve over the next two or three months in an iterative process. Thus, where Shell uses sophisticated computer models to allocate strategic resources across business centers, in Velsicol's matrix an informal version of the same method is used to allocate resources to specific business strategies. Without the aid of computers or fancy mathematics, Velsicol manages to replicate the results of Shell's experience with the strategy matrix.

IMPLEMENTATION

To once more contrast Velsicol with giant Shell Oil, it should be pointed out that Velsicol's strategy managers are also operating managers. Some are product managers responsible for all the strategies that are applicable to a particular product (for example, penetrating the market in one geographic region while hesitating or withdrawing in another). Alternatively, other strategy managers are charged with carrying out a particular strategy that cuts across more than one

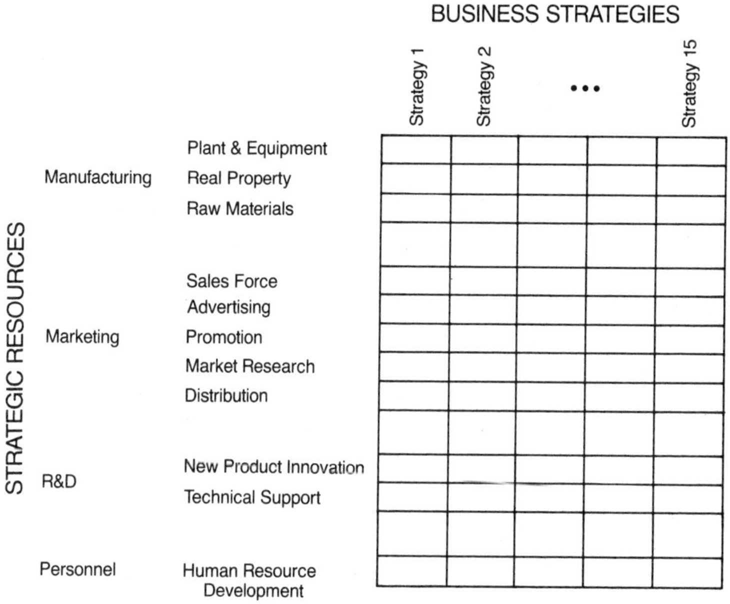

BUSINESS STRATEGIES

Figure 5-1

The Velsicol Business Strategy Matrix

SOURCE: David Barrington, Velsicol Chemical Corporation

product line (for example, office systems productivity improvement). Each strategy manager reports to one of three group vice-presidents, who in turn reports to the CEO. As at Shell, strategic resources, such as manufacturing, marketing, R & D, and personnel, are managed by strategic resource vice-presidents. These vice-presidents report to the CEO, who plays the role of the matrix manager (figure 5-1).

At Velsicol, what the strategy manager is to the business strategy matrix is analogous to what the business manager is to the resource allocation matrix described in chapter 4. In contrast to the strategy managers for the portfolio strategy matrix (chapter 3), who are responsible for strategies that cut across the portfolio of businesses, strategy managers in the business strategy matrix implement strategies within a single business. However, these strategies often cut across a number of functional lines. Although the execution of a specific strategy may require the support of more than one resource manager, the strategy manager retains overall responsibility for coordinating the activities associated with implementing the strategy. With the business strategy matrix, strategic plans are formulated in a matrix structure but are implemented through the various functional organizations. Therefore, the gap between planning and implementation so often found in hierarchical organizations shrinks with the aid of the strategy matrix.

In contrast to conventional business planning, what differentiates the business strategy matrix is that the goals, objectives, and strategies of the resource managers are not determined in isolation. Rather, they are formulated by the whole senior executive group, which typically consists of the senior functional officers of the company. The strategy managers and their respective strategy teams then lock arms with the resource managers to achieve the goals and objectives of their respective strategies. In the event of a conflict between managers, the director of strategic planning intervenes. If mediation fails at that level, the general manager of the company is turned to as referee of last resort.

190

Before the strategies are given final approval by the executive group, it is desirable that the strategy managers meet often with their teams and with the director of strategic planning. These meetings, as well as the meetings of the strategy managers, provide the principal mechanism for managers to respond creatively to the interdependent nature of the strategies and to the fact that they share a number of common resources. Once approved and consolidated into a business plan, strategies ought to be reviewed quarterly at meetings with the strategy managers, who, in preparation for which, should prepare a brief report indicating what progress has been made toward implementation of their respective strategies.

Former CEO Howard Beasley has expressed the opinion that Velsicol's strategy matrix has produced four striking benefits. First, the matrix has made a quick understanding of the company possible, and, second, it has created cohesion among executives with respect to goals and objectives. Third, through the use of the strategy matrix, management has been allowed to spot some "bright stars," and, last but certainly not least, communication barriers have broken down. Fundamentally, what Beasley accomplished in turning Velsicol around was really quite simple. He merely took a traditional functional organization and integrated a set of very well-defined business strategies into the organization. And he did so in such a way as to achieve a maximum degree of cooperation among his functional managers in securing their support of the strategies. Using this tactic, he substituted a divisive zero-sum approach that had almost destroyed the company for a cooperative, non-zero-sum approach to management. Morale improved, productivity increased, and profits responded accordingly. Not only did both strategy and functional managers alike take a more positive interest in their respective jobs, but the new approach offered Velsicol the flexibility it needed to respond effectively to its competitors and to sort out its complex environmental problems. Recently Northwest Industries spun off ailing Lone Star Steel and placed Beasley at the helm as chairman and CEO. Time will tell whether or not the strategy matrix can be used to turn Lone Star around as successfully as was Velsicol.

Other Examples

Federal Express and Florida Power provide us with two more illustrations of the successful implementation of the business strategy matrix. Although Velsicol Chemical, Federal Express, and Florida Power are in three quite different businesses, they independently developed very similar approaches to strategic planning.

FEDERAL EXPRESS

In May of 1982, I happened to be sharing the platform of a professional meeting with Frederick O. Smith, founder and CEO of Federal Express. As Smith began to describe the history of Federal Express and the evolution of its highly successful strategic planning process, it was obvious to me that the way in which Federal Express carries out its strategic planning is very similar to what I had seen at Shell Oil four years earlier. Not only that, but I had recently heard CEO Howard Beasley describe the turnaround situation at Velsicol Chemical. It seemed to me that day that Shell, Velsicol, and Federal Express were all marching to the beat of the same drummer. Although they were each using a very similar approach to strategic planning, they had arrived at its implementation quite independently of each other. The reasons they all gave for adopting the matrix approach to strategic planning were very much the same, however. In each case, overriding concern had developed over the problem of interdependent businesses and strategies in an unstable environment, where high degrees of risk and uncertainty made planning one of the most difficult challenges each company faced. For Federal Express, the risk and uncertainty stemmed from being on the leading edge of airline deregulation and, indeed, anticipating deregulation by several years. Later, when Fred Smith invited me to Memphis to visit the Super Hub of Federal Express, I jumped at the opportunity.

Federal Express Corporation provides overnight, door-to-door delivery of business goods (125 pounds or less) and messages throughout the United States, using its integrated, air-ground transportation system. Other services include second-day delivery and special handling of restricted articles. By mid-year 1984, Federal Express operated a fleet of seventy-six jet aircraft, including thirty-eight Boeing 727s and six

Douglas DC-10s. The company deploys almost five thousand radio-dispatched delivery vans and operates a central sorting facility. Local offices are maintained in over two hundred cities, which are served from ninety-one airports. Each business day, couriers across the United States pick up shipments addressed to consignees in any one of some forty thousand communities. These shipments, in turn, are loaded onto Federal Express aircraft, which then fly, following a hub-and-spokes pattern, to the central sorting facility in Memphis, with most flights arriving between midnight and 1:00 A.M. Goods and messages are unloaded, sorted by destination, and then reloaded onto the aircraft, which return to their points of origin carrying only shipments destined for those areas. Couriers then deliver priority shipments by 10:30 A.M., thus completing the overnight, door-to-door cycle.

Young companies still managed by the original entrepreneurs are rarely noted for their use of formal strategic planning. Ten-year-old, high-flying Federal Express is one of the exceptions. The company utilizes one of the most advanced strategic planning systems in place today in the United States. Under the leadership of Fred Smith, a modified version of the business strategy matrix has been in place at Federal Express since 1974. The matrix is an essential tool in the planning of major new projects, such as the expansion of its international business and the introduction of business service centers, as well as the introduction of its facsimile copier service. The company initiated service to Canada in 1982 and to

Western Europe in 1984. Between those two years, in 1983, Federal Express announced a network of business service centers. These staffed, storefront facilities, of which one hundred new sites were initially planned, are now located in high-traffic, high-density areas. They permit face-to-face contact with many small- or medium-sized customers, many of whom prefer to bring in their packages or documents. All the facilities contain electronic transmitting and receiving equipment and offer business services such as facsimile copying. Specially designed terminals transmit high-quality reproductions with a reliability ensured by the company's satellite-based communications network.

These projects are essentially equivalent to Velsicol's business strategies. They compete with the company's existing businesses—such as Courier Pak and Overnight Letter—for strategic resources, such as flight operations, ground operations, the Super Hub in Memphis, personnel, and maintenance and engineering. Project managers oversee these projects, while strategic resources are managed by senior vice-presidents in much the same manner that Shell and Velsicol operate their versions of the strategy matrix. Although the overnight package business is quite different from either the petroleum or the chemical business, Federal Express finds the strategy matrix to be a viable strategic planning tool. Despite the great difference in the nature of these three businesses, the reasons that Federal Express turned to the strategy matrix were almost identical to those of most of the other companies mentioned in this book. Whether it be the international business, the business service centers, or the facsimile copier service, the business activities of Federal Express are highly interdependent with each other as well as with the company's basic business, which remains the overnight, door-to-door delivery business. Essentially, Federal Express created a totally new business, one that had never existed before, and did it in a rapidly changing regulatory environment where a high degree of flexibility was required. To meet the challenges posed by its ambitious goals and its exciting environment, Federal Express was almost forced to develop a unique approach to strategic planning. Indeed, it is hardly conceivable that Federal Express could have flourished had it employed a traditional, inflexible functional approach to strategic management. It was, and remains, critically important that the functional managers at Federal Express work together in a cooperative manner. The matrix helped facilitate the achievement of the company's goals and objectives.

FLORIDA POWER

When Florida Progress Corporation was created in 1982, Lee H. Scott became president of Florida Power, the lead utility of Florida Progress. At that time, both Florida Power and Scott faced a number of problems, all of a highly interdependent nature. Following the recent completion of Florida Power's Crystal River nuclear plant, the company found itself with excess generating capacity. Florida Power had, however, like many other electric utilities, drastically curtailed its marketing activities in the 1970s. Indeed, it had no plan at all for addressing the problem of excess capacity. Typical of the entire electric utility industry, operating costs at the nuclear plant were running quite high. To cover these high operating costs, the company needed to charge higher rates. But since Florida Power is one of several major electric utilities operating in the state of Florida, the company was being pressured by the Florida Public Service Commission to keep its rates in line with its competition. Furthermore, the fact that the company had recently experienced some erosion of its service area to its competitors provided even further incentive to keep rates down.

It was readily apparent to Lee Scott and his seven-person executive committee, which consists of the senior functional officers of the company, that a functional approach to strategic planning would be virtually impossible to implement because of the complexity and interdependence of the problems facing the company. For example, solution of the problem of excess capacity requires a comprehensive marketing strategy, including a pricing strategy. But a pricing strategy depends on the company's cost structure, the rates charged by competitors, and the attitude of the Florida Public Service Commission. The attitude of the commission, of course, reflects the attitude of the public, and the public is concerned about rates and service. Improved service may cost more to provide, thus necessitating higher rates. It was obvious, then, that the company needed a marketing strategy, a rate strategy, a nuclear power strategy, and a service strategy, not to mention the possibility of strategies that would address human resources, functional problems, public affairs, and matters of corporate citizenship. To assist the vice-president of planning, George Moore, in developing a planning process that would be capable of responding to these problems, Lee Scott invited me to consult with the management of Florida Power. The planning process began in November of 1983, and the first formal strategic plan for the company appeared the following April. Although Florida Power is roughly equivalent in size to South Carolina Electric and Gas, unlike SCE&G, it is a single-business firm, thus making its planning process somewhat more straightforward to design and implement.

The year 1985 marked the third that Florida Power used the strategy matrix as the basis for its strategic management. The planning process at Florida Power follows a format similar to what we have described in other sections of this book. An off-site meeting is arranged each fall for the president and his executive committee, which takes responsibility for defining corporatewide goals, objectives, and strategies. It is in these matters that the real power balancing takes place. To achieve the company's goals and objectives, strategy managers and strategy teams are appointed by the president. In 1984, nine strategy managers and nine strategy teams were appointed. For nearly two months after the off-site meeting, the strategy managers met weekly with the vice-president of corporate planning. They met with him prior to presenting their strategic plans to the executive committee for review and final approval. Recently the company has called on its own in-house organization development staff and on an outside consultant to train strategy managers and members of the strategy teams in the art of matrix management.

Within one year from when it first introduced the strategy matrix, Florida Power turned away from a strategic planning process controlled by one individual toward a participatory planning process involving over seventy-five people. It made the transition from a traditional, top-down management style to a participatory style of management characterized by an extensive use of management teams. No longer are functional managers committed only to their specific area of the company. Rather, strong incentives exist for functional managers to cooperate among themselves and with the nine strategy managers. Although the zero-sum management style of some of the senior managers can still sometimes be seen, much of the initial resistance to the matrix has been overcome. Although it took Florida Power less time to implement the strategy matrix than was the case with SCE&G, the results have been the same: improved morale, improved efficiency, and improved financial results.

In 1985, Florida Power's strategic plan addressed for the first time the sticky issue of rapidly changing supply-side energy technology. Among the technologies identified for mitigating the cost of electric power and new capacity were solar thermal power, photovoltaics, batteries, fuel cells, advanced coal combustion systems, coal gasification, and cogeneration. These topics will no doubt be the subject matter of future strategies as the planning process continues to evolve within the company.

Finally, Florida Power's President Lee H. Scott has summarized the role of the strategic plan as follows:

The strategic plan communicates the objectives that set the direction the Company will take in operating the business. The plan identifies and defines the internal and external environment within which the Company will have to perform. It sets measurable goals which ensure the objectives will be accomplished. The plan will be used as a basis for corporate decisions concerning planning, organizing, and budgeting of resources toward the achievement of the objectives and goals.

Conclusions

When reviewing the use of the business strategy matrix by Velsicol Chemical, Federal Express, and Florida Power, in each case one notices that there appears to have been a very specific reason that the company embraced matrix-oriented strategic planning. At Velsicol Chemical, a new CEO employed the business strategy matrix to achieve the corporate turnaround necessitated by a string of very serious environmental problems. On the other hand, from the very beginning, the matrix formed an integral part of entrepreneur Fred Smith's game plan for making Federal Express an efficient and profitable force in the marketplace. As for Florida Power, its new president Lee Scott saw the strategy matrix as an effective means for consolidating his new management team and leading the company through a difficult transition—from being an independent, stand-alone utility to being the lead utility of its newly created parent company, Florida Progress.

In each of the three companies looked at in this chapter, the business strategy matrix helped break down the functional barriers that had previously existed. The matrix made it possible for the CEO to replace the type of zero-sum mentality often associated with functional organizations with a more participatory approach to strategic planning. All three of the companies illustrated had been organized along functional lines before the business strategy matrix was introduced. Today they remain functionally organized, but their strategic planning takes place in a matrix mode. The common theme underlying the portfolio matrix, the resource allocation matrix, and the business strategy matrix is always the same—matrix-oriented strategic planning with implementation by functional managers.

6

INTERNATIONAL MANAGEMENT: HOW SHOULD WE COMPETE IN EACH COUNTRY?

The Problem of International Management

THE PROBLEM of international management is, in reality, both a recapitulation of and a logical extension of the portfolio problem, the resource allocation problem, and the business strategy problem, all of which were described in the previous three chapters. International management presents itself as a three-fold problem in which the crucial questions to be asked are: What businesses should we pursue in each country? What level of commitment should be made to each business in each country? And how should each of these businesses compete in each country?

The very definition of the problem of international management makes it perfectly obvious that here we are facing a complex multidimensional problem that typically involves numerous countries, businesses, resources, and strategies. The decision as to precisely which countries in which to operate involves multiple economic, financial, political, and social considerations. For instance, ascertaining whether to operate a particular business in a particular country may involve looking at local market conditions, the availability of raw materials, the prevailing wage rate, the type of government, and the type of transportation system that is available in a given country. The level of resources to commit to your business in a particular country will be influenced by all of these factors as well as by the business plan that has been developed for the particular business in question. In addition, the business plan for a specific enterprise in a particular country will draw upon the experience of the business manager in that country.

To state the point quite simply, the problems of international strategic management are far too complex to be managed with the use of traditional hierarchical approaches to planning and management. The standard divisional organization structure fails to address the complexities inherent in the problem of international management. Within a large multinational, multibusiness company such as IBM or Dow Chemical, there are business managers who have worldwide responsibility for a particular business. But there are also country managers for the countries in which these businesses operate, and these people are held accountable for all of the company's operations in a particular country. As soon as we admit the possibility of global business managers and country managers, we have defined a matrix situation. To attempt to force a single-dimensional, divisionalized organization structure onto a two-dimensional problem would seem to be the height of folly, a move guaranteed to fail. We can easily predict that the business managers and the country managers would constantly be in each other's hair with such an unworkable arrangement. If we complicate matters even further and assume the possibility that some resources used by the decentralized businesses in various countries are actually controlled by the staff at corporate headquarters, then the arguments in favor of implementing a matrix are even more compelling.

At one level, the international strategy matrix offers an extremely natural way of accommodating the multidimensional nature of international strategic management problems, much more so than traditional single-dimensional hierarchical approaches afford. Once again, the strategy matrix emerges as a viable option when facing complex business interdependencies. Indeed, it can be argued that when companies attempt to force divisionalized management structures on their international businesses, success comes only by virtue of the fact that informal teams, and, indeed, matrices often emerge among the interdependent businesses and countries. Thus, whether or not senior management formally introduces the matrix into a multinational company, there remains the strong possibility that an informal matrix structure will eventually evolve as a natural response to the multidimensional interdependencies. As will become apparent later in this chapter, the international strategy matrix is more complex than either the portfolio matrix, the resource allocation matrix, or the business strategy matrix. At this point, a word of caution to the reader. Do not confuse the lines of causality and incorrectly conclude that the international strategy matrix is complex because matrix management itself is intrinsically complex. Rather, the problems of international strategic management are complex. The strategy matrix merely represents an attempt to achieve some degree of order in a veritable sea of chaos.

An important conceptual difference underlies the multinational strategy matrix when it is compared with the other forms of the strategy matrix we have described. That is, we must extend to multinational businesses the concept of business strategy that was developed in chapter 5. Again we turn to Michael E. Porter for a useful paradigm for formulating multinational corporate strategies. Porter has suggested four types of global strategies.[1]

Broad line global strategies involve competing on a worldwide basis in the full product line of the industry, capitalizing on the sources of global competitive advantage to achieve differentiation or an overall low cost position. For example, IBM follows this kind of strategy for selling computers, typewriters, copiers, and telecommunications systems in 125 countries throughout the world. IBM's resource allocation matrix, which we described in chapter 4, may also be viewed as a multinational strategy matrix since ten business area managers have worldwide strategic responsibilities. Furthermore, each of IBM's five profit centers has an implicit geographic dimension associated with it. As we previously noted, IBM World Trade Europe/Middle East/Africa controls IBM's operations in eighty countries extending across four continents. IBM World Trade Americas/Far East holds similar responsibilities in forty-five countries, including Australia, Brazil, Canada, and Japan. Although IBM's multinational strategy matrix possesses only two dimensions (profit centers and business areas), all three of the company's global strategic management problems are addressed, that is, portfolio analysis, resource allocation, and business strategy.

When it sold its Far East routes to United Air Lines, Pan American World Airways effectively abandoned a broad line global strategy in favor of a strategy that concentrates on the United States, Europe, and Latin America. On the other hand, Alcoa, Dow Chemical, and Westinghouse each employ broad line global strategies in their respective industries.

By targeting the agricultural chemical industry on a worldwide basis, Velsicol Chemical employs what Porter would call a *global focus* strategy. Rather than trying to be all things to all people, Velsicol targets a particular segment of the chemical industry and then competes in that segment on a worldwide basis.

Alternatively, some multinational companies employ a *national focus* strategy. Here, a company takes advantage of national market differences in order to create a focused approach to a particular national market, thus allowing the company to better its competitors. Although, overall, IBM makes use of a broad line global strategy, in some countries, the company appears to be implementing a highly successful national focus strategy. IBM does extremely well in the United States, Canada, West Germany, and Japan, each of which is a country in which a national focus strategy is used.

Finally, some companies employ a so-called *protected niche* strategy to seek out countries where governmental restraints exclude global competitors by requiring a high proportion of local control in the product, by imposing high tariffs, and so forth. IBM has employed a protected niche strategy in Brazil for many years. Although Brazil has very tough laws restricting the importation of technology into the country, one multinational computer manufacturer consistently enjoys a very high market share in that country's computer market. That company is IBM. There are several distinguishing characteristics about IBM's presence in Brazil. All of the senior managers are Brazilian, for example. Also, IBM has established a major research center in Brasilia and a posh educational center in Rio de Janeiro.

Of the fourteen companies mentioned in this book that are currently using the strategy matrix as a major planning tool, six use the matrix for international management—Alcoa, Citibank, Dow Chemical,

Dow-Corning, IBM, and Westinghouse. Indeed, Alcoa and Westinghouse use the matrix primarily for international strategic planning. We shall now turn our attention to the experience of some of these companies with the international strategy matrix.

Dow-Corning

As Dow-Corning's business continued to expand overseas, it became necessary in the 1970s to add a third dimension to its original two-dimensional strategy matrix (figure 1–2), namely, a geographic dimension, here displayed in figure 6–1.[2] The rationale underlying Dow-Corning's international strategy matrix is identical to the rationale underlying its original resource allocation strategy matrix. Whereas the original matrix was oriented toward the question of which shared resources to allocate to which businesses, the international matrix addressed the question of which resources should be allocated to which businesses in which geographic locations. The issue is no longer just business and shared resource interdependence but rather now includes business, resource, and geographic interdependence.

An important feature of Dow-Corning's multinational matrix stems from the fact that the business and functional managers in the United States have worldwide responsibility for their business or function. Furthermore, over half of the company's worldwide sales are made in the United States, a country in

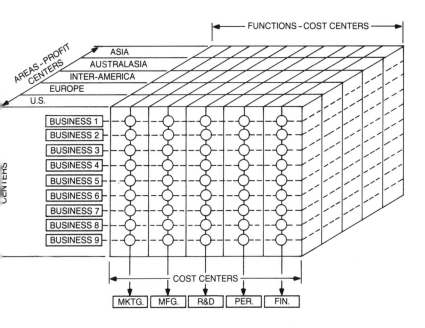

Figure 6-1

The Dow-Corning Multinational Matrix

SOURCE: Robert S. Springmier, Dow-Corning Corporation

which the matrix is fully operational. A similar matrix is in place in Europe, where the business and functional managers in each country report to the manager of the European area; they also report to their worldwide counterparts in the United States. The areas outside of the United States—including Canada, Latin America, and the Pacific—are currently in the process of developing their own matrix structures.

When Dow-Corning introduced geographic areas into its strategy matrix, the company's strategic planning process (described in chapter 1) was modified accordingly. Not only are profit plans now required for each business, they are also required for each geographic area. Thus, geographic area managers must cooperate not only with the functional managers from whom they obtain their resources but cooperate with business managers as well. In the Dow-Corning multinational strategy matrix, *business managers* assess external opportunities and internal capabilities for their product line, develop five-year objectives and strategies consistent with opportunities and capabilities, and propose specific programs to implement strategies. *Area managers*, on the other hand, assess social, political, and economic factors in their countries, develop one-year sales and profit targets for their area, reconcile strategic proposals of businesses with short-term profit goals, and develop operational plans for the coming year.

Functional managers establish key functional standards of performance, make uniform planning assumptions, advise businesses on alternative functional programs, and prepare detailed cost-center budgets for approved programs. The *corporate planning department* develops, documents, and operates the planning system, provides resources for analysis of the external environment, and analyzes planning proposals from businesses, areas, and functions. The department then makes recommendations concerning these proposals to the executive committee. Finally, the *executive committee* reviews and approves proposals by functions, businesses, and areas to en-

sure that they represent acceptable performance, acceptable probability of success, and a satisfactory allocation of resources.

More recently, the executive committee has become more directly involved in the process of allocating strategic resources. In the past, resources were allocated to functions and to businesses, but the committee used the matrix to allocate resources to specific projects and programs. Lately, the executive committee has begun to review a selected list of programs quarterly. The funding of all major programs is reviewed as an integral part of the planning process, which contributes directly to reshaping the portfolio of businesses.

The international strategy matrix is merely one more step in the continuous evolution of Dow-Corning's strategic management process, which began with a functional approach to strategic management, evolved into a divisional approach and then into a matrix approach. In assessing Dow-Corning's fourteen years of experience with the strategy matrix, in 1982 Robert S. Springmier, then director of corporate planning, had the following to say:

Although it has taken several years, we are now satisfied that the strategic redirection we needed is being accomplished. Whereas our sales have doubled in the last five years, we have about 25 percent fewer products in the line. We have a higher concentration of strategic effort in major programs, and we believe that they are well defined, well managed, and realistic.

211

Alcoa

Alumina, ingot, sheet and plate, electrical conductor, and chemicals are but some of the businesses Alcoa is in. The products of these businesses are manufactured and sold on a worldwide basis. Aluminum ingot, for example, is produced in six foreign countries with four different sets of business partners; it is also produced in the company's U.S.-based facilities. In some areas of business, such as the production of refined aluminum oxide (which is the feedstock for metal production), capacity at the foreign affiliated plants is more than half of Alcoa's total system capacity. The company no longer enjoys the luxury of single ownership in any one country nor the inherent homogeneity of goals, objectives, and simplicity that such an arrangement permits. With multiple international business partners, each with a unique set of cultural, legal, and political attributes, traditional single-command planning systems do not provide the necessary flexibility to survive in the complex multinational environment. Therein lay the rationale underlying Alcoa's use of the international strategy matrix.[3]

As was the case with Dow-Corning, to appreciate the use of the strategy matrix at Alcoa, it is necessary to review the evolution of the company as an organization over the past fifty years, especially since the end of World War II. It comes as no great surprise to us to learn that Alcoa's growth during World War II was rapid. The end of the war found the company highly decentralized but focused almost exclusively in the United States. Alcoa had no operations outside of this country other than raw material supplies in the Caribbean region.

By the early 1950s, however, there was a strong movement to bring together the various decentralized elements of the company in order to achieve a highly centralized organization structure. Faced with increased competition, Alcoa rationalized that a move toward centralization would provide a unified sense of direction to the various segments of the business so that new markets could be identified and that the expanded capacity created during World War II would be more fully utilized. Basically, the company evolved into a classical functional organization structure similar to the one in place at Dow-Corning in the early 1940s. At that time, corporatewide manufacturing reported to one senior executive and corporatewide sales, and marketing reported to another, both of whom reported to the CEO. During this period in Alcoa's history, the company maintained a large corporate staff and evolved uniform corporate policies that were implemented throughout the company. In addition, most of the company's lines of business were very closely related, and priority was placed on economies of scale and efficiency of operations.

Alcoa began to diversify in the early 1960s into a number of different finished products, and for the first time since the 1920s, expanded its overseas operations. At the same time, the highly centralized functional organization structure began to ease into a more divisionalized organization structure. As divisions came into existence, decentralization most often occurred along major lines of business. However, many of the staff functions of the company remained centralized at the corporate headquarters. Simultaneous to these developments in the early 1960s, the company was pursuing increased flexibility. It did so by decentralizing marketing and manufacturing and economies of scale with regard to other corporate resources, such as accounting, engineering, and legal services. For example, a central engineering staff provided support to all of Alcoa's operating divisions. Management had to learn to balance priorities in a two-dimensional organization structure that consisted of operating divisions and shared resources. At the same time, Alcoa continued to expand its international operations, and as these foreign operations continued to grow, they developed a strong sense of autonomy, resulting from such causes as geographic remoteness, cultural differences, and complex ownership patterns. Greater decentralization meant that now the company had to cope with a variety of different types of relationships between the central corporate staff and the various divisions and foreign operating units. So, by the mid-1960s, we find in place all of the necessary underpinnings for the birth of the strategy matrix at Alcoa.

During the 1970s, Alcoa moved even further in the direction of divisionalized operations by continuing to expand overseas. Major installations for primary metal and aluminum were developed in numerous countries to serve global markets for these products. And in the 1980s, we are witnessing more of the same kind of development.

In the 1983 Alcoa annual report, CEO Charles W. Parry outlined six long-term challenges faced by the company: (1) the cyclicity of the aluminum business; (2) rising power costs; (3) increased price volatility with the trading of aluminum as a commodity; (4) the increase in government-owned or influenced facilities as a percent of total primary aluminum capacity worldwide; (5) slower growth in aluminum consumption in the United States, the world's largest market for aluminum; and (6), which is perhaps most important, the relentless threat from competitive materials. To address these challenges and maintain Alcoa as a viable, competitive force in the international aluminum industry and the global marketplace, the company's senior management has defined three fundamental strategies aimed at achieving long-term profitable growth in Alcoa's worldwide operations:

1 Strengthen our aluminum core. The aluminum core comprises bauxite and alumina, primary aluminum, and flat-rolled products—the foundation on which the Company was built.
2 Enter new areas and expand existing businesses that build upon our strengths. One of the Company's key strengths is a technological capability in materials— in alloy development, in Formica, joining, coating, and finishing metals and in composite materials.
3 Increase productive contributions through greater

individual participation, competitive economic rewards, and a work environment that encourages creativity, initiative, and trust.

To meet the company's long-term challenges through the implementation of these three competitive strategies, Alcoa recently adopted the international strategy matrix. William H. Hoffmann, manager of Organization Planning for Alcoa, has summarized the reasons that Alcoa has moved toward the strategy matrix:

Major non-U.S. investments by Alcoa have grown into large companies with sophisticated facilities serving sophisticated markets. They are truly competitors in their own right in the worldwide economy. To be successful, therefore, these units need the same level of technology, the same level of management competence and skills as do the company's U.S. facilities. At the same time, these investments are important to host country economies, and they often have local partners in the ownership. These offshore entities have become part of a worldwide system which has multiple sources for any given product. Therefore, the total system must be balanced and optimized by utilizing alternative sources to supply specific markets. To achieve this, matrix relationships have evolved.

Let us now summarize a few of the important elements in Alcoa's international strategy matrix and report on some of its experiences with the matrix.

GEOGRAPHIC DIMENSION

Alcoa employs a dual command system to plan and manage its international businesses. The lowest common denominator in this system is the single-operating company. For example, in Great Britain, Alcoa owns an affiliate company that operates rolling mills to produce sheet and plate goods. If there exists more than one legal entity in a country, such as is the case in Great Britain, then some kind of countrywide coordination among the Alcoa affiliate companies in that country may be needed. Country managers are appointed to provide this type of direction and support. In the case of operations in a number of closely related countries, such as in Western Europe, there may also be a need for regional management.

Basically, the geographic dimension of Alcoa's multinational matrix is concerned with the unique characteristics of the culture and host governments of the affiliated companies in a particular country or region. From an organization standpoint, both country and regional managers report to Alcoa's international department in the corporate headquarters in Pittsburgh. The head of the international department reports directly to the president of Alcoa.

BUSINESS DIMENSION

The second dimension of Alcoa's international matrix, the business dimension, focuses on the linkage of the operating companies that produce the same product or products, each of which may have different ownership and be geographically separated. In the case of Alcoa's British affiliate, it is one of several worldwide sources of sheet and plate products within the Alcoa system. Sometimes it is convenient to cluster similar businesses under a group manager. Business management inputs to Alcoa's British affiliate company flow from the company's mill products department in Pittsburgh. This department also reports to the president of Alcoa. The business dimension of Alcoa's matrix attempts to address a number of business management questions, such as: What products should the company produce? Which markets should be entered? How should products be produced? It is the responsibility of the general manager of an individual operating company to integrate the business inputs from the business management dimension of the matrix with the geographic dimension.

EXPERIENCE

According to William H. Hoffmann,

The key to making the structure work is agreement on objectives and priorities. Both sides have long- and short-term objectives. The dilemma of the individual company manager is to keep both bosses properly informed, to alert them both to possible conflicts in terms of their direction and, if possible, help find a way for them to reach an appropriate balance.

As the balance within Alcoa has shifted from the company being a heavily U.S.-oriented organization to one with substantial overseas activities, Alcoa has found that American predominance is no longer so great that its foreign operations occupy only a minimal role. In summary, Hoffmann notes that

Instead of a U.S. parent telling its foreign children what to do, we have several brothers and sisters, each with their own ideas, who have to work as a team. Therefore, we are encouraging the managers of our various companies to get together regularly, to identify issues, and jointly develop solutions which will optimize the interests of all parties. The key to finding solutions to date seems to stem from careful planning and strategies, identification of alternatives, and very good personal relationships built up over the years between the managers. Without calling it a matrix, our management has made both parties jointly accountable.

Dow Chemical

Dow Chemical Company's international strategy matrix lies at the heart of the company's diversification program, which was begun in 1978.[4] Dow initiated this program as a result of the many changes that have affected the chemical industry during the past ten years, a decade that began with the 1973 oil embargo and ended with the worst worldwide recession in over fifty years. In light of this turmoil, Dow's senior management agreed that a major change in corporate strategy should be enacted to guarantee continued long-term earnings growth. After careful consideration of supply and demand forecasts for basic chemicals and plastics, which are the mainstays of its business, Dow's management opted to establish a diversification objective "to generate consistently 50 percent of the Company's earnings from value-added products and services by the 1980s." These products offer high-growth potential and reduce the company's exposure to economic downturns. With the aid of the international strategy matrix, Dow is vigorously pursuing this diversification in all of its operating areas throughout the world. Although acquisitions do have a place in Dow's strategic plans, for the most part the company intends to build on existing product know-how and technological strength.

In no sense does Dow intend to yield its premier position as a manufacturer of basic chemicals and plastics. Says Hunter W. Henry, executive vice-president and president of Dow Chemical U.S.A., "We are redeploying our resources, not abandoning basic chemicals and plastics. We will devote the R & D and capital expenditures required to maintain our leadership position in those products." The criteria for deciding if a product is a so-called specialty product go beyond product volume. Dow's specialty products usually involve proprietary technology, patent protection, or unique properties that give them a specific niche in the marketplace.

To accomplish its diversification objective, Dow has formulated the following four specific strategies to expand the specialties segment of its product mix:

1 Increase management attention and resources devoted to existing specialty products.
2 Extend successful value-added products to all possible operating areas.
3 Identify new market needs and develop products to meet these needs.
4 Accelerate the pace at which new products are developed through research.

By way of an overview of the company, Dow invents chemistry-related products, manufactures them in plants in thirty different countries, and sells them from sales offices in sixty-one countries. To achieve its ambitious diversification objective, Dow makes use of a three-dimensional international strategy matrix consisting of six geographic areas, three major functions, and over seventy products.

GEOGRAPHIC DIMENSION

Dow is decentralized geographically into six autonomous operating companies with headquarters in Hong Kong, Brazil, Canada, Switzerland, Florida, and Michigan. The corporate headquarters is located in Midland, Michigan. Each operating company has its own marketing, manufacturing, research, and various administrative functions. With over one hundred manufacturing sites located throughout the world, it is easy to see that planning and organizing such a complex operation require a nontraditional organization structure.

FUNCTIONAL DIMENSION

The *functional dimension* of Dow includes the three primary business functions of marketing, manufacturing, and research. One of the challenges facing a high-technology company like Dow is the transfer of technology to units located all over the globe. A second challenge, according to corporate planning director Roger Gohrband, is, "to ensure that innovations and improvements in technology are communicated and implemented throughout the world regardless of where they originate." This is accomplished at Dow through manufacturing technology centers and global R & D coordinators.

Manufacturing technology centers can be found at a specific plant location where the particular product is manufactured. The technology center manager, who is also a senior line production manager, has a separate technology center staff to deal with all aspects of the particular technology, including assessment of competitors' technologies. The global R & D coordinators (who are actually called global product technical leaders) are also line managers. They provide worldwide research leadership for large product families and coordinate global R & D priorities on those products to meet the needs of the six geographic areas. They also attempt to minimize duplication of effort and to measure progress toward established R & D targets. A recent addition to managing R & D in Dow's matrix is the naming of ten global product development specialists to assist in introducing certain specialty product families outside the United States.

PRODUCT DIMENSION

The *product dimension* of Dow's multinational strategy matrix (aside from agricultural products and pharmaceuticals) is managed by the Global Product Management Unit, which is headed by one of Dow's three executive vice-presidents. Five product vice-presidents develop and manage Dow's global product strategies across all geographic and functional lines.

Agricultural Products and Pharmaceuticals each have an even stronger global product management thrust, with a corporate group vice-president and an executive vice-president heading them. These two product groups each have their own line research effort, and to some extent, line manufacturing and commercial organizations on a global basis. This results in what some would call a "mixed matrix," with two line organizations operating globally alongside the geographic, functional, and product matrix.

Within each geographic area, commercial product departments are profit centers and are charged with the overall management of a group of businesses. Business managers within these departments are responsible for product strategies, for developing business and product management teams, and for involving key people from each function to serve on and contribute to those teams. These teams are pivotal to the success of the strategy matrix at Dow.

MANAGEMENT TOOLS

To ensure that the product dimension of the strategy matrix receives adequate attention from the functions and geographic areas, five basic tools are available to the product vice-presidents: strategic planning, capital budgeting, reporting, pricing, and product balances. Strategic plans are formulated for about seventy major product families on a worldwide basis. Each product vice-president is responsible for a group of product families. The product vice-president utilizes a global network, which is made up of business managers in the various geographic areas, each of whom develops individual product strategies and financial forecasts based on agreed-upon global product strategies. These strategies are reviewed at least annually and updated as needed. This global network of business teams both communicates and meets frequently to review long-term strategies. They also scrutinize short-term problems and opportunities.

Dow is a very capital-intensive company. In each geographic area, capital investment is managed against a capital budget that is derived from the product programs each region wishes to implement. Program approval requires the support of the product vice-presidents. The objective is to generate programs that are consistent with the company's strategic goals and to avoid duplication of programs throughout the world. Product vice-presidents also become involved in major business ventures or contracts that require substantial capital commitments or that involve more than one geographic area.

An integral part of Dow's strategy matrix is its global reporting system, which generates a periodic income statement showing global sales and profits by profit center and geographic area.

A fourth analytical tool used by Dow's product vice-presidents is a floor-pricing system for the company's major globally traded products. This pricing system exists to provide a uniform policy on important pricing issues. The system does, however, have the flexibility to grant exceptions when they are warranted.

The final analytical tool relied upon at Dow is a

product balancing system that attempts to balance supply and demand for the company's products on a worldwide basis.

EXPERIENCE

Dow's 1983 annual report summarized some of the results to date of the four diversification strategies that are being implemented through the strategy matrix:

1 *Increase Management Attention and Resources Devoted to Existing Specialty Products.*

The 1970s was a decade of geographic expansion for basic chemicals and plastics that required large amounts of capital and close management attention. Consequently, many specialty-type products did not receive the management attention or the financial resources necessary to support rapid growth. There were exceptions such as epoxy and latex businesses. This strategy, although simple, was designed to help the exceptions become the rule.

Starting with the Pacific Area, each Dow operating area has reorganized its commercial operations to provide the appropriate support for both commodities and specialties. "A primary objective was to create an organization that allows Dow to act like a small company," says Paul F. Oreffice, president and chief executive officer. "Each business must be able to act quickly, and somewhat independently."

Some of these businesses may integrate line functions into an independent unit, including separate compensation programs and career paths. In 1983, Dow Canada established one such business unit to service the construction industry. Says Oreffice, "We are working to provide the organizational flexibility needed for Dow to be competitive in specialty markets."

"A lot is expected from our specialty business units," says Oreffice. "That's why we have placed successful, top-notch managers in charge who know how to get the job done."

Accompanying the increase in management attention is an increase in financial resources. Research and development expenses devoted to the specialty area have risen 72 percent since 1980, double the increase devoted to basic products. The percentage of Dow's capital expenditures directed at these products has also increased.

2   *Extend Successful Value-added Products to All Possible Operating Areas.*

Dow's worldwide organization will help the Company profit from its investment in specialty products and services. The U.S. Area generated more than 60 percent of the profits in these product groups during the last five years. Now Dow's existing geographic organization is extending that success to other parts of the world. For example, Styrofoam insulation is now manufactured on four continents and marketed in 53 countries. New plants in Australia, Spain and Saudi Arabia will extend Styrofoam products into even more markets.

The possibilities for implementing the second diversification strategy are numerous. The maturity of Dow's European markets make the area particularly well suited for line extensions, while Dow's operations in Canada, Latin America, Brazil and the Pacific are positioned to introduce existing products from the U.S. and Europe.

3   *Identify New Market Needs and Develop Products to Meet Those Needs.*

Understanding the needs of Dow customers and the ultimate consumer is essential to identifying new product opportunities. This "outside-in" approach to innovation is the third strategy for achieving Dow's diversification objective.

Dow's geographic diversity gives the Company a unique capability to identify local opportunities for diversification. For example, Dow Latin America launched Kuron herbicide for pasture applications in Colombia, while Dow Europe started commercial introduction of Starane, a broad-spectrum herbicide for cereal grains.

4 *Accelerate the Pace at Which New Products Are Developed Through Research.*

Taking ideas from the chemist's bench to commercial status is generally a long, arduous process. Speeding up that system is the last major strategy for generating more profits from specialty products and services.

Much of Dow's research effort has been focused on three areas of high business potential—pharmaceuticals, agricultural products and plastics fabrication. This targeting of resources helps the R & D organization quickly identify and develop commercially viable products.

Providing a development avenue for new products is essential to accelerated research. And Dow is organized to meet this need in each of its operating areas. If a new product does not have a ready fit with Dow's commercial organization, the discovery, development, and innovation development functions of Dow are responsible for moving the idea rapidly through the Dow system. An internal venture may be formed to obtain the support from marketing, sales and technical service required to make the critical transition from research to commercial status. One such internal venture for hollow fiber membrane technology led to the formation of the Cynara Company in 1981.

Roger Gohrband has succinctly summarized the three factors he feels have most contributed to the success of the strategy matrix at Dow:

First, our geographic organizational units permit the delegation of decision making to the lowest possible levels as individual competence is demonstrated. Out in the world is where the action is, and where our Dow people best know the territory. It's hard to second guess that from a seat on the banks of the Tittabawassee River [where Dow's corporate headquarters is located].

Second, we insist on strong functional expertise across the whole organization. On the technical and scientific side, this is fostered by our manufacturing technology centers and global R & D coordinators.

Third, on the commercial side, strategic product direction and short-term coordination are managed by product vice presidents working with cross-functional teams of key people located in each geographic area.

Westinghouse

In February of 1983, Westinghouse was reorganized into three groups: Commercial, Energy and Technology, and Industries and International. The Industries and International Group, which uses the strategy matrix, provides products and services to industrial, construction, and utility markets globally. It also serves as the principal channel for Westinghouse business activities abroad. In 1979, John C. Marous, Jr., now president of the Westinghouse Industries and International Group, was asked by the senior management of Westinghouse to undertake a comprehensive study of the international marketplace and to find out what would be required to enable Westinghouse to survive and prosper on a worldwide scale.[5] The study, conducted by a task force consisting of sixty-five of Westinghouse's top executives and professionals, generated the following conclusions:

1 In the eighties, real economic growth will be much higher in the developing countries than in the U.S. and other countries. To achieve real growth, Westinghouse must expand its already substantial international presence and "go where the action is."
2 Competition is getting stronger and more global in scope. More companies around the world are abandoning the concept of "home market" and are thinking, planning, and acting on a worldwide scale.
3 The individual country, with its unique cultural, political, and economic characteristics, is the main strategic element in the organization of a successful multinational corporation.
4 Success in the international marketplace will largely depend on the Company's ability to dovetail its country-oriented planning and operations with its product-oriented planning and operations.
5 Technology is the key to penetrating world markets and it is also one of the greatest strengths of Westinghouse. Eighty percent of the Company's product lines have characteristics suited to international trade. The challenge is to orient the Company's

planning to take these lines and develop products to meet the specific needs of the country in which they will be used.

All of these conclusions seem to add up to one thing for Westinghouse International Marketing and Strategic Resources Director Alan J. Meilinger, "that it was time for Westinghouse to reorganize its international operations in a way that would bring product management and geographical management into focus simultaneously." What was recommended by the task force was an evolutionary transition to an international matrix management system that would bring about a gradual "cultural" change within the corporation.

The fundamental building block of Westinghouse's international strategy matrix is the *country.* Operations within each country are jointly managed by the *country manager* and the *business unit manager;* the two will share decision making, accountability, and financial results. Country managers, of which there are sixteen, have a similar relationship with every other business unit manager involved in their country. Most business unit managers work with several country managers around the world. The business unit manager and country manager carry the heaviest burden of shared responsibility and decision making. According to John C. Marous, Jr., "Their interface is the tie rod that holds the matrix together and makes it work." Figure 6–2 attempts to summarize the responsibilities of the Westinghouse business unit managers

LEAD RESPONSIBILITY		SHARED RESPONSIBILITY
Business Unit	Country Management	
1. World product strategic planning & implementation	1. In-country strategic planning & implementation	1. Nature of in-country presence
2. World product sourcing	2. Marketing	2. In-country subsidiary management
3. World pricing	3. Support services	3. Product support
4. Product technology	4. Corporate representation	4. Project management
5. Human resources	5. Human resources	5. Human resources

Figure 6–2

Westinghouse International Matrix Responsibility Chart

SOURCE: John C. Marous, Jr., Westinghouse Electric Corporation

and country managers as well as to illustrate their shared responsibilities.[6]

The business units take the lead responsibility on worldwide product strategic planning and implementation, including the scope of core product lines; product-line additions; product standardization; and product rationalization. World product sourcing and world product pricing are also lead responsibilities of the business units. Product technology—including research, design, development, and manufacturing processes—are lead responsibilities of the business units. However, country management is expected to provide valuable inputs on in-country standards, applications, and appropriate technologies. For example, the Power Circuit Breaker division of Westing-

231

house planned and developed a circuit breaker for worldwide marketing that was actually developed by the company's affiliate in Spain.

Country managers are held accountable for strategic planning, its implementation, and the integration of all in-country Westinghouse activities. Countries where this process is currently at work include Brazil, Spain, and Korea, where in-country plans have been developed with the active involvement of business unit personnel. Country management also takes the lead when in-country marketing decisions must be made; this includes sales channels and organizations, distribution policies, and the selection of special sales representatives. In Brazil, for example, Westinghouse has approved the creation of a single specialty sales organization whose task will be to meld the sales forces from several of the company's divisions into one highly effective unit. Among the other support services that are the responsibility of country managers are such activities as cash management, order entry, in-country office facilities, and communications. Country managers are the senior Westinghouse officials in their country and have the lead responsibility for corporate representation. The country manager coordinates all in-country representation activities, including government relations and public relations. The country manager must balance the political, legal, economic, competitive, and market forces that may affect the company's performance in that particular country.

Defining the nature of the Westinghouse presence within a country is the shared responsibility of the business unit manager and the country manager. For example, these two managers jointly evaluate the opportunities for exports, in-country manufacture and investments, and licensing to local companies. Management of in-country subsidiaries is also a shared responsibility. Subsidiary managers report to both the business unit manager and the country manager, thus making them jointly responsible for setting objectives, financial goals, strategies, and the investment levels for their subsidiaries. Their performance is measured accordingly.

The subsidiary manager is responsible for in-country pricing and in-country terms and conditions of both corporate core products and special products that are not manufactured in the United States. However, in-country pricing and terms conditions must be consistent with the pricing policies and practices established by the business unit. The business unit manager and country manager share responsibility for product support, including field engineering, after-sales service, and spare-parts supply. Jointly they also manage in-country projects that are outside the scope of the company's nuclear or defensive operations.

Finally, human resources is an across-the-board function. Business unit management and country management have individual and joint responsibilities for this important function. The most important joint responsibilities involve the selection, development, and compensation of key personnel in the in-country subsidiaries. These people must work with both the business unit manager and the country manager. Since such personnel are a shared human resource, both sides of the matrix must be happy with them.

After the reorganization of the Industries and International Group in 1983, three key strategies were defined for the group. First, business units will expand their array of world-class products. Second, greater use will be made of global product sourcing, including joint ventures and technology exchange. Such arrangements will generally lead to greater U.S. exports. And third, operations within the group will be rationalized. In the process, offices and factories will be streamlined and further automated. Sophisticated inventory control systems will be introduced to increase profitability. Common engineering and marketing centers and joint component-manufacturing facilities will be established. These strategic moves are anticipated to create a more efficient global network of production and distribution.

The Westinghouse Industries and International Group currently uses the strategy matrix to implement these strategies. The company's international strategy matrix rests on the following four principles:

1. Definitions of specific responsibilities must be sufficiently flexible to accommodate the great diversity of Westinghouse products and markets.
2. The degree of involvement of the country managers and the business unit managers will vary from country to country, from product to product, and with time.
3. The responsibility chart is not carved in stone. It can be modified as experience dictates. The ultimate

test is: What is best for Westinghouse Electric Corporation?

4   Westinghouse has three "special situation" businesses—nuclear, defense, and Thermo King—that require a modified responsibility chart.

As the strategy matrix of Westinghouse continues to evolve, management has identified five stages through which country matrices have evolved in those countries where they have been implemented:

1   *Market Development.* The country strategy focuses on export improvement, business development, and building a coordinated approach to the customer in the field.

2   *Strategic Entry.* The strategy shifts from opportunistic to more long-range considerations; establishing a coordinated country strategic plan, a focal point for the company's presence, and good relations with the government of the host country.

3   *Transition.* The strategy aims at boosting market penetration, at increasing country operating profit, and at refining and developing the strategic planning capability.

4   *Consolidation.* The strategy centers are consolidating three or more operations and a number of country functions with a view toward strategic growth and increased country operating profit.

5   *National.* The strategy establishes the country as a company with its own goals and resources—a fully self-supporting entity. The growth strategy is almost entirely country driven.

While in the process of summarizing Westinghouse's experience with the international strategy matrix, one senior executive told me, "We are learning to do business amid vast political, social, and economic changes that are revolutionizing the international marketplace. Our international matrix gives us a unique means of ordering the apparent chaos of world markets and transforming that chaos into future profitability."

Conclusions

In this chapter, I have described the experiences five very diverse companies have had with the multinational strategy matrix. These companies included a manufacturer of silicones, a giant computer manufacturer, an aluminum company, a large chemical company, and a manufacturer of electrical products. Three of these companies—IBM, Alcoa, and Westinghouse—deploy two-dimensional matrices to their strategic planning activities. IBM's strategy matrix consists of ten multinational business areas and five profit centers. Alcoa and Westinghouse, on the other hand, have created a version of the strategy matrix whose dimensions are businesses and geography. Dow-Corning and Dow Chemical each utilize three-dimensional multinational strategy matrices, with geography, functions, and businesses or products as the matrix dimensions.

The principal force underlying the adoption of the multinational strategy matrix by all the companies discussed seems to be the need they have experienced for increased flexibility as they attempt to compete successfully in the international marketplace. That American multinational companies are looking for more effective ways to compete in new markets abroad should come as no surprise when one considers the following facts: America's trade deficit in 1984 was nearly double the record $69.4 billion deficit recorded for 1983. Increased foreign competition, a strong dollar, and the severe import restrictions imposed by Third World nations aggravate the problem. Although this country's economy recovered substantially in 1983 and 1984 from the worst recession in fifty years, many of the so-called smokestack industries did not participate in the recovery.

The multinational strategy matrix has not only provided increased flexibility for multinational companies, it has also provided a mechanism for increased cooperation among country managers, business managers, and functional managers on a worldwide basis. Furthermore, one must remember that multinational companies are by no means immune to the problems of interdependent businesses and interdependent functions that have been discussed throughout this book. On the surface, the three-dimensional strategy matrices of Dow-Corning and Dow Chemical may seem quite complex. The reader should keep in mind, however, that the matrices are not the cause of the organizational complexities of these companies. Rather, these complex matrices merely reflect the degree of complexity that pervades large multinational companies. The multinational strategy matrix simply provides a tool for cutting through some of the enormous organizational complexities that plague firms like Alcoa, IBM, and Westinghouse.

Whether talking about the portfolio problem, the resource allocation problem, the business strategy problem, or the problem of international management, the philosophy underlying the application of the strategy matrix to each of these problems is always the same, namely, a multidimensional strategic planning process combined with a functional approach to implementation. As is always the case, the power of the matrix lies in its ability to encourage cooperation and teamwork among business managers, functional managers, country managers, and strategy managers. Indeed, that is the common denominator underlying the application of the multinational strategy matrix by each of the five companies described in this chapter.

7

MANAGERIAL

IMPLICATIONS OF

THE STRATEGY MATRIX

Corporate Culture

AS WAS STATED in chapter 1, the culture prevailing within a particular corporation is a strong determinant of whether or not the strategy matrix can be effectively implemented within that organization. The term *corporate culture* refers to the overall ambience existing within a company, including the attitudes and customs of its management and employees. It is not by chance that the strategy matrix has succeeded at companies like IBM, Intel, Shell Oil, and Federal Express, companies that have very strong people-oriented cultures, and that it has failed in, for example, a larger, impersonal, and bureaucratic New York-based insurance company. A major electronics firm that lacked a clear sense of direction for the thousands of engineers and technicians it employed can also be noted as a company whose culture undermined the successful implementation of the strategy matrix.

In his recent book, *High Output Management*,[1] the founder and president of Intel, Andrew S. Grove, describes the corporate culture at one of the nation's premier high-technology companies, in fact the fourth largest in the U.S. semiconductor business. Intel employs over twenty thousand people and is known for its strong commitment to matrix management. Through the use of an informal management style characterized by the extensive use of teams and matrix management, Intel creates an atmosphere for its employees that is conducive to personal growth and achievement. Although Intel's management has a reputation for being tough and demanding, the company nevertheless challenges its employees and provides an environment in which achievers are motivated to excel. And employee motivation is maintained by constant monitoring and recognition of achievement by one's peers.

Through the use of matrix management, Intel attempts to bypass the adverse effects of traditional hierarchical organizations and their attendant bureaucracies. The company places considerable emphasis on innovation and creativity by management and employees alike. For instance, to maintain Intel's flexibility while remaining alert to changes in technology, worker councils have been grafted onto the twenty-five SBUs that are involved in product planning. In this way, planning is allowed to cut across functional lines within the company. Built into the corporate culture at Intel is a desire to reduce the distinctions that exist between the various groups of employees as well as between employers and management. Intel has discarded formal enclosed offices and instead now makes use of flexible, partitioned work areas, with special attention given to equity across these work areas. Intel's participatory management style provides for special privileges for its executives but no special office facilities. Furthermore, the company dictates no dress code, and there are no reserved parking areas.

Corporate culture is shaped by at least two important factors—the external environment of the firm and the philosophy of management of the senior executives of the company. Just as our own personalities are shaped by our parents and by the environment in which we were raised, corporate culture cannot help being influenced by the social, political, economic, and religious environment of the firm. If corporate culture, however, was determined solely by the external environment, with no possibility for the intervention of the will of senior members of the firm, then management would be deprived of one of its most challenging and exciting opportunities, namely, actually influencing corporate culture. Furthermore, if outside forces were the only source of influence, then the possibility of altering the corporate culture in such a way as to make it compatible with the strategy matrix would be precluded. The principal instrument available to senior management for influencing the corporate culture is the company's philosophy of management.

One definition of "philosophy" is that it is an analysis of the fundamental principles underlying conduct. A philosophy of management thus is concerned with basic principles underlying the conduct of the affairs of a business. The aim of a firm's philosophy should be to provide meaning and direction to the managers and employees of the business. A philosophy of management that is well thought out will influence the goals and policies of a company as well as its management style, each of which in turn then helps shape the nature of the company's culture.

The rationale underlying the need for a philosophy of management is aptly captured by a line from Tennessee Williams' play *The Glass Menagerie*: "Man is by instinct a lover, a hunter, a fighter, and none of those instincts are given much play at the warehouse." Perhaps the reader's reaction to these words is the same as was mine when I first came across them. "How true it is!" I thought. And, I believe it is because these instincts have been so thoroughly ignored by corporate strategists that so many corporate giants are now foundering aimlessly in a sea of economic chaos. When leaders have no sense of meaning or direction in their personal lives, how can they possibly motivate employees to climb on board a leaderless ship?

Although every company does possess a philosophy

of management, usually one finds that it has not been written down on a sheet of paper and circulated to the employees. Few companies, in fact, have actually taken the trouble to identify their corporate philosophy in writing. But the failure to formulate the company's philosophy of management can lead to confusion and misperception on the part of second- and third-generation managers, who, more often than not, have missed any personal contact with the original entrepreneur of the company, a person who probably had a quite strong and even forceful unwritten philosophy of business.

I am not surprised, however, that so few companies circulate formal philosophies of management. Indeed, it can be argued that senior management finds it more difficult to formulate a philosophy of management than to devise a strategic plan. Yet, I think it fair to ask: How can any company implement a meaningful strategic plan to which there is across-the-board commitment if the company's philosophy of management is weak and ill defined? How can management know what it is buying into if the values of the CEO are unclear, or, worse yet, devoid of meaning?

While the company's philosophy of management is an important determinant of the company's culture, it would be remiss not to acknowledge the likely possibility that the inverse is also true: that culture influences the philosophy of management as well, particularly in those cases where senior management has been in place for a long time. However, even if senior management has been ensconced for many years, in a free society any firm still retains the right and the personal freedom to change its beliefs and its values. Without such freedom, the whole subject of corporate philosophy loses meaning and thus would have no place in a book such as this, which is devoted to a specific planning system whose success depends on management's ability to integrate it into the company's culture. Essentially, the idea we are proposing is that the company's philosophy of management is process-oriented and that it is the critical driving force in the company's culture. The corporate culture, on the other hand, can be described as being both attitudinal and action-oriented. These attitudes and actions, however, are shaped primarily by the company's philosophy of management as well as by the impact of the external environment on the company.

An interest in corporate culture must be threefold. First, we need to determine to what extent corporate culture influences the possible acceptance of the strategy matrix as an alternative to the existing planning system. That is, will it be possible to convince senior management to back a matrix-oriented approach to strategic planning? Second, we must ask how the corporate culture will affect the implementation of the strategy matrix. That is, what currently existing characteristics of the company will either enhance or interfere with the implementation of the matrix? Finally, we are also interested in the extent to which the implementation of the strategy matrix in a company may actually change the corporate culture.

Managerial Implications of the Strategy Matrix

Obviously, an approach to strategic planning that depends on cooperation, trust, participation, and team building, which is what characterizes the strategy matrix, is not likely to be accepted in a corporate culture whose values are in conflict with these fundamental assumptions. What if the corporate culture is actually hostile to the value system on which the matrix is based? Is it possible to change the culture, and if so, how does one go about doing it? From the fourteen companies surveyed in this book, I believe there exists strong evidence that it is indeed possible to change the culture of a company, but that such change is often accompanied by some shock in the external environment and/or a change in the senior management.

Consider the case of South Carolina Electric and Gas. The matrix was implemented after a merger and a corporate reorganization by its new CEO, Virgil C. Summer. Before he installed the matrix, Summer relayed some very clear signals that he intended to change the corporate culture of SCE&G. For example, two women and a black man were promoted to vice-presidencies—for the first time in the company's history. One of the two women later became vice-president of governmental affairs. In a very short period of time, she replaced the company's very traditional special interest lobbying program with a completely open and participatory government education program that won the respect of the state legislature and the South Carolina Public Service Com-

245

mission. This new level of trust between the state government and the company resulted in a favorable decision on the part of the Public Service Commission concerning the company's request to increase its electric rates to cover the costs of its new nuclear plant. These events indicate for all to see that clearly there has been a change in the company's values and its culture. The rigidity and inflexibility characteristic of the past have given way to cooperation, flexibility, and fairness, and the new corporate officers have contributed to a greater sense of community in the company.

Unfortunately, the types of values outlined above are rarely exhibited in most hierarchical organizations. Senior executives who take great pride in their self-sufficiency, independence, and frontier view of society may remain unconvinced to buy the cooperative approach that underlies the strategy matrix. So-called theory X managers, who are known to be aggressive, competitive, forceful, and threatening in their managerial style, are hardly likely to cotton to the strategy matrix.

IMPLEMENTATION

The two most important cultural factors influencing the successful implementation of the strategy matrix are the commitment of the CEO and organization flexibility. Without exception, in each of the companies mentioned in this book, it was the strong commitment of the CEO to matrix-oriented strategic planning that was of critical importance to the successful implementation of the strategy matrix. If its number one advocate is not the CEO, the strategy matrix does not stand a chance!

Large, inflexible bureaucracies—such as government agencies, state universities, and AT&T (before its breakup)—rarely make good homes for the strategy matrix since organization flexibility is an absolutely essential element in the implementation of the matrix. According to Stanley M. Davis and Paul R. Lawrence,

> . . . some organizations have cultures that are more hospitable to a matrix than are others. If there is a strong tradition of rigid bureaucracy, minimal contact even when called for, a belief in the sanctity of reporting lines, etc., then even if the nature of the organization's activity calls for a matrix, it is unlikely that one would be successful unless the culture of the organization was also changed.[2]

The implementation of the strategy matrix at Velsicol Chemical Corporation in 1978 was accomplished, you will recall, with a completely new management team. Prior to that time, Velsicol had been plagued with what appeared to be an endless stream of environmental and legal problems arising from its production of the two flame retardants PBB and Tris, and a pesticide, Phosvel. In 1978, however, the team of strategy managers was headed by a new CEO, one who held strong legal, academic, and governmental credentials. And since most of the strategy managers were relatively young, they were eager to help turn the company around. Whereas the previous management had tried to camouflage the seriousness of the company's problems, the new team displayed a refreshing openness and flexibility and seemed not at all inhibited by traditions of the past. I firmly believe that it would have been impossible to implement the strategy matrix under the direction of the previous management and its value system.

IMPLICATIONS

Thus far, I have argued that the corporate culture has to be "right" in order for the senior management to buy into the strategy matrix and for it to succeed. But the very act of introducing the strategy matrix into an organization is likely to bring about cultural changes and possibly even culture shock. For example, when the multinational strategy matrix was introduced at Alcoa and Westinghouse, it was obvious that one of the objectives was to encourage management to put aside some of its traditional isolationist views and adopt a more open, outward view of the world. Some functional managers at SCE&G and Florida Power felt very threatened when the strategy matrix was imposed upon their hallowed departmental turf. Some even resigned.

Perhaps the most dramatic example of the use of a matrix-like approach to strategic management as an instrument of cultural change is the reorganization of General Motors, which was announced in January 1984. As you may recall from chapter 1, General Motors is moving away from the notion of five independent automobile divisions, an idea that was conceived back in the 1920s by the company's legendary chairman, Alfred P. Sloan, Jr., and is moving today toward a consolidation into two new groups—a small-car group and a large-car group. According to Cary Reich in the *New York Times*,

> The guiding principle behind it all was to increase the decision-making power of staff at every level of the company and to loosen the chain of command. In a broad sense, this was accomplished by giving the two divisions total control of the cars they produced. On a more down-to-earth level, subordinates were given more direct access to their bosses. "I have 15 people reporting to me now," says Lloyd E. Reuss, head of the Chevrolet-Pontiac-GM Canada (small-car) group. "In the past, it would have been eight or nine."

> The new approach meant that top management could more clearly determine who deserves credit or blame for a particular decision—reward the successful managers and root out the unsuccessful. And it had another key advantage. "Participative management," as the program was labeled, gave workers the chance to make more decisions, to play a larger role in reaching decisions. It can be, as Reuss points out, "an important motivation in bringing out new ideas in people."[3]

Since the reorganization began, there is more attention devoted to innovation and creativity than ever before. Chairman Roger B. Smith has successfully challenged the corporate culture of the giant monolith. "He is presiding over a top-to-bottom internal reorganization—shaking up the company's formidable bureaucracy, demanding that its staff become more venturesome, more outward-looking, more entrepreneurial."[4] That is a lot for an $84 billion company to absorb in a relatively short period of time. There is little doubt who is managing the corporate culture at General Motors today. His name is Roger Smith.

The cultural changes brought about by the strategy matrix are soon mirrored in the behavior of individuals and groups within the organization. Additional knowledge, new attitudes, improved interpersonal skills, and greater energy levels are among the necessary attributes of matrix managers. Because of the large amount of flexibility inherent in the strategy matrix, individuals within the matrix are likely to experience a much higher degree of freedom than they enjoyed in the past. But along with this freedom comes a dramatic increase in responsibility. Sadly enough, this combination of increased freedom and increased responsibility can sometimes generate heightened anxiety for matrix managers. This phenomenon was particularly noticeable at SCE&G and Florida Power when the strategy matrix was first introduced there. The newly appointed strategy managers expressed great insecurity in their new roles. The prospect of interacting directly with senior officers in other areas of the business loomed as very threatening. But training and the strong commitment of the CEO in both of these companies helped pave the way to an increased level of confidence on the part of the strategy managers.

Anxiety can either be constructive or destructive. When it is constructive, anxiety stimulates and can enhance a person's creative abilities and energy level. On the other hand, as Rollo May has pointed out, "The anxiety that comes from excess freedom can also be destructive in that it can paralyze us, isolate us, and send us into panic."[5] Indeed, the challenge of matrix management is to provide an environment that is conducive to constructive anxiety, the kind that will lead to higher levels of achievement and personal growth for all of the members of the matrix team. In a number of cases, the careers of business managers and strategy managers who have been involved with the strategy matrix have literally skyrocketed toward the top of the organization.

Team Building

Through a multiple command system and team building, the strategy matrix seeks to instill constructive, cooperative, non-zero-sum behavior into organizations that previously were characterized by their destructive, competitive, zero-sum behavior. In a matrix organization, whether one is a strategy, business, resource, or country manager, team building is the key element for success. Teams make up an integral part of the corporate culture of matrix-oriented companies like Shell Oil, IBM, Intel, and Federal Express.

The transition from a hierarchical, single-command system to a multicommand matrix often proceeds along a very bumpy road. Definite answers to some of the very difficult questions posed by matrix team members are required, thus necessitating frequent pauses along the journey. For example, managers want to know how the team will be organized, who will lead it, and what the responsibilities of the team members will be. They will also ask about the objectives of the team and what methods will be employed for making decisions. And what about conflict resolution among team members? How will managers identify the responsibilities they have to the departments in which they reside? Last, and perhaps most important of all, the question must be addressed as to how the team's performance will be judged. Not only team performance, but how will individual team members be rewarded? Formulating answers to these questions will not be easy, but to a great extent the answers will depend on the degree of cooperation and trust that exists within the matrix and how conflict resolution is handled among the team members. These two topics are important enough to warrant further exploration.

COOPERATION AND TRUST

Throughout our discussion we have described many different kinds of teams—portfolio strategy teams, business teams, business strategy teams, and country teams. Regardless of the nature of the team, however, considerable importance to the success of the team is that an attitude of cooperation and trust be established among individual team members, between the team and the person to whom the team is responsible, between the team and other related teams, and, last, between the team and departmental bosses to whom individual team members report for those activities that take place outside the team. To illustrate what I mean by an attitude of cooperation and trust, let us consider People Express Airlines, a company that has achieved an impressive financial track record since it began flying in 1981. According to Sara Riner in the *New York Times,* the company bases its entire philosophy of management on a matrix-oriented team approach.[6] Not only has this approach engendered enormous cooperation and trust among the company's employees, but senior management has learned that people work harder and enjoy their work more if they are provided with four basic things: a financial stake in the company, an opportunity to learn and hold a variety of jobs, an organization that allows workers to make decisions based upon a company philosophy and tradition, and a sense of belonging, not just to a company but to a family.

For the strategy matrix to work, a high level of trust must exist among members of the team. If the attitude is guarded and if members hold back important information that is relevant to the business or to the strategy, then the entire exercise in team effort is doomed to failure. Members must be open about the conflicts they feel between loyalty to their respective functional areas and loyalty to the team. It is the job of the team leader to create an environment in which team members feel free to share information about their attitudes, views, and personal feelings. Among the values to be strived for are unity, cohesiveness, team spirit, trust, sharing, and commitment. Experience at Florida Power, SCE&G, and Velsicol Chemical suggests that these are the values more often associated with women than with men. Whereas male managers often seem egocentric and obsessed with the need to be in control of all situations, women, who are traditionally more accustomed to providing nurturance, seem to find it easier to work in organizations where interdependence is valued and respected. Women managers appear less self-centered than do their male counterparts and therefore may find adjustment to participatory management systems such as the strategy matrix much easier. The fact that women are usually less competitive, less aggressive, and therefore are perceived as less threatening greatly facilitates their ability to function in a matrix organization. Without exception, all of the female strategy managers at each of the aforementioned companies were particularly effective.

Members of a matrix team must also, if they hope to be effective, be willing to take risks and to communicate openly with other members of the team. They must be prepared to reveal more about themselves and their true attitudes about the business strategy or the project than they have been accustomed to doing in the past. The perceived risk involves exposing one's self and not being certain whether other team members will respond in kind or whether one will simply experience a loss of control. These points can be illustrated by the experience of SCE&G with its initial set of strategy managers, all of whom were senior functional officers of the company. For the most part, the strategies they proposed called for maintaining the status quo. None of the managers wanted to rock the boat for fear of disturbing their own turf. However, the following year, these strategy managers were replaced by a group of younger middle managers who were less averse to risk. A whole new set of creative strategies was the result.

The strategy matrix also demands substantial problem-solving skill on the part of members of the matrix teams. In many ways, these managers are forced to emulate the analytical and cognitive skills normally associated with senior management. They must assimilate information from a variety of sources within the organization and then make judgments under stress, a reaction to pressure emanating from the different stakeholders in the organization. The unique thing about the problem-solving skills required in a matrix organization is that these skills are needed by more people at much deeper levels in the organization than is usually the case with hierarchical organizations. Florida Power was particularly fortunate to have the vice-president of engineering as the manager of the planning process that included training the strategy managers. His problem-solving orientation was an invaluable asset to the entire process.

CONFLICT RESOLUTION

Regardless of the type of matrix organization, the number of contacts between individuals is likely to be substantially higher than is found in functional organizations. The interdependencies characterizing matrix organizations simply generate a much greater need for communication among individuals. But the

255

increased need for communications created by the multiple command system of the strategy matrix also increases the possibility of conflict. In hierarchical organizations, conflicts are resolved when individuals take their problems to their individual superior. But in a matrix organization, in which there are multiple bosses as well as team members who come from different functional organizations, one would want to avoid using the overall matrix boss to resolve routine conflicts. Otherwise, the common boss would soon be overloaded with relatively trivial decisions. Generally speaking, individuals within the matrix should be encouraged to solve their problems and disputes within the matrix rather than resorting to the general manager of the matrix.

One premise underlying the strategy matrix is that a certain amount of interpersonal conflict may be a sign of a healthy organization. Corporations in which everyone agrees with everyone else are often rigid or inflexible and soon die. The real trick to good matrix management is in using conflict creatively to arrive at solutions to problems that would not otherwise have been even considered in hierarchical organizations. Creative conflict resolution implies openness, honesty, and flexibility. Those individuals who are preoccupied with power and control make poor matrix managers because they are always trying to manipulate other individuals. Intel and People Express present noteworthy examples of matrix-oriented organizations where effective conflict resolution systems are built right into their management teams.

Organization Development

The introduction of the strategy matrix into an existing organization is, in itself, an act of organization development. For example, in single-business companies like Velsicol Chemical, Federal Express, and Florida Power, the matrix was introduced into highly centralized, functional organizations to introduce a greater degree of flexibility and to reduce some of the zero-sum management conflicts that characterize such organizations. On the other hand, when the strategy matrix was introduced at Shell Oil, the company was organized as a highly centralized, multibusiness functional organization. The role of the matrix was to introduce some balance between the company's portfolio of businesses and its critical resources. Whether a company is organized functionally or along divisional lines, the introduction of the strategy matrix represents a move away from excessive centralization in the direction of decentralization.

Matrix management creates a demand for improved human resource planning as well as management and organization development. An effective matrix requires input from managers with experience in overseeing each of the dimensions of a matrix. For example, the general manager of an international matrix such as Westinghouse's should have experience in managing businesses and resources as well as in managing the operations of a particular country.

257

It is imperative to stress here how important it is that future matrix managers be given multidimensional management experience if they are going to be expected to assume the responsibility of managing a matrix. Thus, a future-oriented corporation will automatically assure that a system for identifying potential matrix managers will be established within the organization. In addition, having in place a management development plan to prepare these managers for their future responsibilities is of primary importance.

PLANNING PROCESS

Whether a company is organized as a matrix or not, a close relationship should exist between the strategic planning process and the organization development function of the company. Indeed, without a strong organization development plan, it can be argued that formal strategic planning is virtually impossible. Organization constraints often present the most serious impediments to the successful implementation of formal strategic planning. In fact, it is hardly an overstatement to suggest that organization development must pave the way for the introduction of formal strategic planning. And when the planning system in question is the strategy matrix, it is even more imperative that organization development and strategic planning march in unison.

STAFFING

Most companies that adopt the strategy matrix staff their matrix with individuals from within the organization. While Velsicol Chemical is an exception, IBM and Shell Oil routinely do so. The strategy matrix does, however, possess its own unique staffing requirements. The importance of effective deployment of human resources cannot be underestimated, especially given the multiple command system of the strategy matrix and the potentially large number of individuals involved in its implementation. Positioning the right kind of people in the proper slots at the right time necessitates a substantial commitment to human resource planning. Further matters that ought to be of concern to the company are succession planning and the training of new matrix managers. Florida Power, for example, made extensive use of an outside organization development consultant as well as its own human resource department to deal with both of these issues.

Given the level of trust that is required in a matrix organization, the flow of individuals in and out of the matrix must be completely open. For instance, Shell Oil often brings people at lower levels into the matrix in order to groom them internally rather than rotating more senior people through the matrix. Older functional officers often seem to find it extremely difficult to adjust to the multiple command system of the strategy matrix. One creative approach to this kind of problem was devised by SCE&G. The company established a "voluntary" early retirement program when it implemented the strategy matrix. Needless to say, many potential conflicts were avoided by this tactic.

One aspect of staffing that is often overlooked is

the relative quality and status of the individuals along each dimension of the matrix. For the matrix to be successful, positions must be balanced. For example, in a business strategy matrix, if all resource managers are senior vice-presidents and all strategy managers are junior managers, we can hardly anticipate a stable working relationship. Admittedly, balance is extremely difficult to achieve during the early stages of the evolution of the strategy matrix. Dow-Corning, however, tackled this problem at the very outset by giving equal status to business and to resource managers. On the other hand, this issue continues to be a nagging problem for the electric utilities that employ the strategy matrix.

There is one final staffing implication of the strategy matrix to note. With matrix management, the traditional distinction between line and staff functions becomes quite blurred. Although both business and country managers are clearly operating line managers, a case can certainly be made for the assertion that strategy managers and resource managers are line managers as well. These distinctions between line and staff managers become increasingly vague, however, the longer the matrix is in place, as is the case at Dow-Corning, IBM, and Shell Oil.

CAREER PATHS

Not to be overlooked is the impact that the strategy matrix has on the career paths of matrix managers and members of teams associated with the matrix. There are two important considerations. First, everywhere it has been used, the matrix has proven itself to be an effective means of providing comprehensive on-the-job training for both line and staff managers. As mentioned before, it is common within many companies—IBM and Shell are two examples—for line or staff people to rotate through the matrix before being reassigned to a new position outside of the matrix. By pushing decision making deeper into the organization while simultaneously broadening managers' participation in decisions, the matrix provides valuable training for those involved in its inner workings.

In addition, the matrix provides some unique challenges in terms of the options available for promoting effective matrix managers. On the one hand, while the matrix broadens the number of positions of authority within the company, a decision must be made as to whether a "promotion" implies movement within the matrix or movement to another line or staff position. In a hierarchical organization, it is much easier just to structure positions so that managers are rewarded by promotion to the next level in the hierarchy. The absence of such a hierarchy makes this task much more of a challenge in the matrix. At Velsicol Chemical, to cite one case, one matrix manager's career really soared after he used the matrix to achieve a corporate turnaround. In less than five years from the time he introduced the matrix at Velsicol and became its CEO, William Howard Beasley, III, was promoted to executive vice-president and then president of Northwest Industries, the parent company of Velsicol Chemical. Not surprisingly,

three other operating companies of Northwest Industries soon began using the strategy matrix—Lone
Star Steel, NWT Resources, and General Battery.

COMPENSATION

Any compensation system that might be designed
for matrix managers is subject to two serious complications. First, since matrix management is by definition team management, it is almost impossible to sort
out the contributions made to the strategy, business,
or country operations by individual team members.
Second, given the high degree of interdependence
that exists among most strategies, businesses, and
projects, determining which team within a matrix deserves which share of any rewards that may be allocated may be very difficult. Obviously, the design of a
matrix management compensation scheme involves a
host of practical, ethical, and accounting issues. Although it is beyond the scope of this book to provide a
detailed treatment of management compensation
systems, we shall at least attempt to define some of
the important issues.

At the heart of the matter is the extent to which the
company believes in the concept of individual accountability and what attempts it is willing to make
to assign costs and benefits to individual managers
within a matrix organization. In the previous
chapters, we have pointed out how difficult it is to
assign fixed costs to interdependent businesses and
business strategies. We noted that Shell Oil does not

attempt to assign fixed costs to those businesses that share common refineries. On the other hand, Velsicol Chemical does allocate costs by strategy, even though the allocation formula it uses is somewhat arbitrary.

Any matrix management compensation system should consider at least four factors: company performance, matrix performance, team performance, and individual performance. In setting incentive pay for individual matrix managers, the individual manager's contribution to the job, to the team, to the matrix, and to the company as a whole must be carefully weighed. A strategy manager, for example, may be judged on how long it took the strategy team to accomplish its goals and objectives, or by how much outside assistance was required. Judgment may be made on the basis of whether costs exceeded the budget, or how effective interpersonal relations were. A resource manager, on the other hand, might be judged on the basis of staffing, training, directing, and development of the particular resource organization. All of the strategy managers and resource managers in a two-dimensional business strategy matrix, for instance, might be judged on the profitability of the company's operations as well as on the conditions under which the financial targets were achieved. Performance evaluation might well be based on such questions as: What were the conditions in the company's external environment? What obstacles had to be overcome to achieve the financial results?

At several companies, including Florida Power and SCE&G, the implementation of the strategy matrix necessitated a complete review of the executive compensation program. In each case, numerous changes were made to bring the compensation program in line with the multidimensional nature of the matrix. A related problem that can arise is how to reward strategy managers when the results of a strategy may not be measurable for two or three years in the future. An example of one response to this kind of problem comes from Velsicol Chemical. CEO Howard Beasley developed a control system and an executive compensation plan based on degree of strategy implementation rather than on short-run operating results. Thus far, it appears that the strategy managers at Velsicol are reasonably satisfied with this compensation scheme.

Management Systems

Although the primary emphasis of this book has been on multidimensional strategic planning, such a planning system is obviously not the only management system that is required in order to support most large, complex organizations. Equal in importance to strategic planning are budgeting, accounting and control, and decision support systems, which, in a mature strategy matrix, should all be multidimensional systems. Although it is obviously not practical to bring all four of these management support systems on line simultaneously when the strategy matrix is first implemented, managers should be aware of the requirements of each of these systems as the matrix evolves.

Consider, for example, the resource allocation matrix (chapter 4), whose dimensions are businesses and resources. Not only should each business control its own budget, but the major functional resources should have budgets as well. Basically, the sum of the resources allocated across the portfolio of businesses should be equal to the resources available. Just as double-entry accounting double counts everything, so it is with a dual-budgeting system. In a similar fashion, there should also be a multidimensional accounting and control system to support the strategy matrix.

Resource budgets are primarily cost budgets. They begin with each business team's estimates of the requirements of each critical resource and are usually estimated in work hours, material requirements, or percentages of capacity utilization. Resource managers then add indirect costs and overhead charges to these direct costs to arrive at the price that will be charged to the businesses for each specific resource. Business team managers may either accept or reject these internal prices. Challenges to the internal resource prices are usually accompanied by threats to go outside the company to acquire a particular resource. Once the internal resource prices are accepted by the business teams, it is then possible to compute pro forma income statements for each business. The budgets for specific businesses, business strategies, and countries are driven by the strategic plans of each of these respective matrix dimensions. Resource budgets, on the other hand, are governed by the resource requirements of the strategic plans defined along the other dimensions of the matrix.

Finally, to support multidimensional planning, budgeting, and accounting systems, one needs a computer system or so-called decision support system that can operate along multiple dimensions as well. With the exception of Velsicol Chemical, all of the companies using the strategy matrix possess some type of computer-based modeling system that enables them to evaluate the effects of alternative strategies on the behavior of a single business or on the entire company. Given a forecast of the company's external environment, these computer-based modeling systems are used to conduct various "what if?" experiments in order to evaluate individual strategies or various combinations of strategies. A variety of different computer hardware and software options are currently available for doing this type of analysis. The options range from large computer mainframes to small, desktop microcomputers, as well as to various combinations of these two approaches, which are sometimes called distributed processing computing. Inadequate computational power is not a serious deterrent to the analysis of strategies within the context of the strategy matrix. However, an inability to conceptualize some of the complex interdependencies that arise in the form of computer models is a real limitation of decision support systems. Shell Oil has by far the most sophisticated computer-based multidimensional planning, budgeting, and accounting system currently in operation among those companies using the strategy matrix.

Interpretation of the Strategy Matrix

When we step back and examine the fourteen organizations currently using the strategy matrix, we notice that they are an extremely diverse lot with regard to size, industry, organization structure, and applications of the strategy matrix. They vary in size from Velsicol Chemical and Dow-Corning, with annual sales of less than $1 billion, to Federal Express, Florida Power, Intel, and SCANA, whose sales approach the $1 billion mark, to multibillion-dollar giants like IBM and General Motors. Among the industries represented by this group of companies are aluminum, banking, chemicals, silicones, air cargo, public utilities, automobiles, computers, petroleum, pharmaceuticals, and electrical. Over half of the companies using the strategy matrix are large multinational, multibusiness companies operating on a worldwide scale. Dow Chemical, General Motors, and IBM are examples that immediately come to mind. Velsicol Chemical is an operating company of Northwest Industries. Shell Oil is the American subsidiary of Royal Dutch Shell; and Dow-Corning is jointly owned by

Dow Chemical and Corning Glass. Federal Express, Florida Power, and Velsicol Chemical are to a great extent single-business companies.

All of the fourteen companies are profitable, and some, like IBM, General Motors, and Shell Oil, are very profitable. Federal Express, Intel, and IBM are considered to be high-growth companies, while Dow Chemical, Velsicol Chemical, Florida Power, and SCANA are in more mature industries. As can be seen, the diversity of the companies using the strategy matrix is unquestioned.

In terms of applications of the strategy matrix, SCANA and Squibb use it for corporatewide portfolio planning. Indeed, SCANA was actually conceived by the portfolio strategy matrix at SCE&G. On the other hand, Dow-Corning, Shell Oil, IBM, and Squibb employ the resource allocation strategy matrix to allocate shared resources across a portfolio of interdependent businesses. Single-business companies such as Velsicol Chemical, Federal Express, and Florida Power apply the business strategy matrix to problems of business strategy. International management is the primary focus of the multinational strategy matrices of Alcoa, Citibank, Dow Chemical, and Westinghouse International.

The four problems defined in chapter 1 represent a set of common problems that underlie most of the applications of the strategy matrix. They include business interdependence, zero-sum management practices, management alienation, and organization inflexibility. These problems were shared by virtually all of the companies that have adopted the strategy matrix.

In this book, I have reported on all of the examples of the strategy matrix with which I am familiar. Undoubtedly there are other companies either currently using this approach to strategic planning or that have used it in the past. However, I suspect that the number of such companies is quite small.

In addition to the obvious financial success enjoyed by the companies that use the strategy matrix, it may be useful to recapitulate some of the other dimensions of the success of these companies, particularly those accomplishments that can be directly linked to the strategy matrix. IBM used the matrix to help navigate itself through the turbulent waters of the 1970s, years agitated by the long-standing antitrust suit held over the company's head by the U.S. Justice Department. Throughout this period and continuing into the 1980s, IBM chalked up record sales and profits. While I would hesitate to suggest that the strategy matrix was the cause of IBM's impressive record, surely it helped!

When General Motors reorganized in early 1984, the company introduced a matrix approach to strategic planning and effected a new set of large-car, small-car strategies. As reported in the *New York Times*, GM also created some important new business strategies, including (1) buying more parts from abroad, (2) accelerating automation and shrinking employment even further, (3) buying high-tech companies to enhance know-how, (4) importing Japanese subcompacts for sale as GM models, and (5) producing compacts in the United States through a joint venture with Toyota.[7]

On the other hand, Velsicol Chemical achieved a complete corporate turnaround in record time by ridding itself of some very serious environmental and legal problems and focusing on agricultural chemicals as its primary business. Indeed, one of its main strategies was to free itself of its past environmental problems.

Alcoa, Dow Chemical, and Westinghouse International adopted the strategy matrix in order to increase both their flexibility and their ability to compete in international markets. The matrix was used by Federal Express as a tool for forging important new growth strategies, including the introduction of new products and services. The matrix was also the instrument SCE&G used to facilitate a merger with a gas company, a corporate reorganization, the licensing of its nuclear power plant, and the creation of SCANA Corporation, a new holding company. By 1985, SCANA Corporation and Florida Progress, the holding companies of SCE&G and Florida Power respectively, had become two of the most cash-rich utilities in the United States.

In firms receptive to cooperation, trust, and team building as a philosophy of management, the strategy matrix may not only be a powerful participatory approach to strategic planning but also an effective instrument of change. Furthermore, it has stood the test of time. Several companies—Dow-Corning, IBM, and Shell being sterling examples—possess over ten years of experience with the strategy matrix. Not only does the matrix work, it works very well.

The Future

I believe that the strategy matrix is applicable to a wider variety of different types of organizations, both large and small, than those described in this book. Surely the strategy matrix should be suitable for financial institutions of all sorts; consulting firms, hospitals, universities, religious organizations, as well as for all levels of government. When the World Corporation Group of Citibank's International Banking Group was established in 1974, it was organized as a matrix. It was created to deliver a full range of services to the bank's 457 multinational corporate clients, which are located throughout the world. The dimensions of the matrix included multinational corporate clients and specific countries. The matrix succeeded so well in the World Corporation Group that it soon spread to other activities within the International Banking Group.[8]

In many ways, large financial institutions appear to be ideal candidates for the use of the strategy matrix. Given the high level of interdependence existing among the functional activities of banks, insurance companies, brokerage houses, and others, adoption of the matrix would seem to be a logical move for these companies. Yet, with one exception—Citibank—relatively few financial institutions possess any experience whatsoever with the matrix. If one reflects on the dimensions along which an international bank like Citibank is organized, the potential applicability of the matrix is immediately apparent. For example, geography, types of customers, products and services, and resources make up the important dimensions of management for Citibank.

Federal, state, and local governments in the United States also face most of the same problems experienced by the corporations that have turned to the strategy matrix. For example, waste in government often stems from the fact that competing agencies frequently duplicate the services they offer. This point is best illustrated by the way in which the armed services are organized in this country. The military is divided into four relatively autonomous services—army, navy, marines, and air force—each of which is supported by separate but very similar support functions. Although bureaucrats in the Pentagon would no doubt put up a great deal of resistance, the strategy matrix could be of substantial benefit to the U.S. Defense Department.

Alternatively, the objectives of some government agencies are diametrically opposed to those of other agencies. Consider the case of cigarette smoking. The Surgeon General's Office and the National Institutes of Health spend millions of dollars each year warning the public about the hazards of smoking tobacco. At the same time, the U.S. Department of Agriculture provides numerous programs aimed at improving the productivity and profitability of tobacco farmers.

Why shouldn't the government set goals, objectives, and strategies just as the private sector does? Shouldn't it, as well, have a mechanism to manage the planning and implementation of the programs required to support its objectives? Again, the strategy matrix would appear to be a viable alternative to the current chaotic state of affairs.

Recently, considerable interest in the strategy matrix has been expressed by a number of state-owned enterprises in Eastern Europe, enterprises that are becoming more decentralized and more market-oriented. Several Hungarian enterprises, for example, have begun using the strategy matrix as they make the transition from being under strong centralized state control to an environment in which the approach to business is more decentralized and market-oriented. Most of the large state-owned, multiproduct firms in Hungary were organized as highly centralized functional organizations until recently. As economic reform continues to push decision making deeper and deeper within Hungarian enterprises, the strategy matrix offers Hungarian managers a powerful tool for coping with multiple products in a decentralized environment. For example, BVK, the second largest chemical company in Hungary, recently used the strategy matrix to develop and implement a strategy involving the introduction of a major new product. Under Mikhail Gorbachev, similar economic experiments are now taking place in the Soviet Union. That is, highly centralized state-owned enterprises are gradually becoming less centralized and more market-oriented. Soviet managers with whom I have met have also expressed a strong interest in the possible applicability of the strategy matrix to the restructuring of Soviet enterprises. Indeed, this is not surprising since the strategy matrix is essentially ideologically neutral. It is a tool to help managers find the right balance between top-down and bottom-up plans. For this reason, it may have equal appeal to managers of firms under capitalism as well as socialism.

In spite of the favorable track record logged by the strategy matrix, the corporate culture of some American companies may not be quite ready to accept this approach to management. But during the past ten years, "Japan watching" has become a favorite pastime of American executives who are concerned about competition from this tiny island nation. It is important to point out that an ingredient to the success of Japanese companies seems to be the team approach to management that is routinely used. Japanese firms place strong emphasis on cooperation, trust, and group performance. These are precisely the values most commonly associated with the strategy matrix! As American managers become more aware of the benefits of participatory management systems, the strategy matrix will no doubt also grow in popularity.

Regardless of the corporate culture, few companies, large or small, have escaped the four problems that provide the rationale upon which the strategy matrix is based: business interdependence, zero-sum management, alienation, and inflexibility. As most companies continue to grow, these problems typically become more pronounced. Thus, as these problems increase, it can be predicted that corporate culture in the United States will become more receptive to participatory management practices. The strategy matrix may thus be predicted to find a much larger corporate audience. Furthermore, the relatively low-key pace at which it has evolved since 1968 may bode well for the future of the strategy matrix in an era that has seen management fads come and go at an alarming pace. The strategy matrix has passed the test of time and experience by some of the largest and best managed companies in the United States. It may not be a cure-all for every type of management ailment, but it certainly can be called a very effective planning management system.

NOTES

Chapter 1

1. Among the companies that are known to be using the strategy matrix are Alcoa, Citibank, Dow Chemical, Dow-Corning, Federal Express, Florida Power, General Motors, IBM, Intel, Shell Oil, South Carolina Electric and Gas, Squibb, Velsicol Chemical, and Westinghouse International.

2. Phillippe Haspeslagh, "Experience with Portfolio Planning: The Result of a Survey," in *Portfolio Planning and Corporate Strategy*, Thomas H. Naylor and Michele H. Mann, eds. (Oxford, OH: Planning Executives Institute, 1983), p. 51.

3. John Naisbitt, *Megatrends* (New York: Warner Books, 1982).

4. John Simmons and William Mares, *Working Together* (New York: Knopf, 1983).

5. "A Train of Disasters for Nuclear Power," *New York Times*, January 22, 1984, sec. 4, p. 24.

6. Alvin Toffler, *The Third Wave* (New York: Bantam Books, 1980).

7. Naisbitt, p. 76.

8. Thomas J. Peters and Robert H. Waterman, Jr., *In Search of Excellence* (New York: Harper & Row, 1982), p. 15.

9. Ibid., p. 307.

10. Ibid., p. 314.

11. Ibid., pp. 20–21.

12. The companies that were using some form of matrix management during 1979–1980 include Boeing, Dow Chemical, General Electric, General Foods, Hewlett-Packard, IBM, Intel, Lockheed, Rockwell, Texas Instruments, and Westinghouse.

Chapter 2

1. John Naisbitt, *Megatrends* (New York: Warner Books, 1982), pp. 192–93.

2. Stanley M. Davis and Paul R. Lawrence, *Matrix* (Reading, MA: Addison-Wesley, 1977), pp. 16–17.

276

Notes

Chapter 3

1. "General Electric Strategic Position: 1981," Harvard Business School Case 9-381-174, President and Fellows of Harvard College, 1981 (revised March 1982), p. 6.
2. Thomas H. Naylor, *Strategic Planning Management* (Oxford, OH: Planning Executives Institute, 1980), pp. 59-65.
3. Ibid., pp. 65-74.
4. Bruce D. Henderson, "The Experience Curve—Reviewed" (leaflet), The Boston Consulting Group, 1974.
5. Ibid.
6. Naylor, pp. 75-77.
7. Jerome M. Waldron, "Strategic Management: An Application of the Multiproduct Firm Behavior," Ph.D. dissertation, Duke University, 1983.

Chapter 4

1. The general formula for net present value (NPV) is given by:

$$NPV = \sum_{t=0}^{T} \frac{R_t - C_t}{(1 + i)^t},$$

where NPV = net present value,
R_t = revenues received in year t,
C_t = costs paid for in year t,
i = rate of interest, and
T = length of the planning horizon for the project.

As an example, suppose that one of the businesses of a particular company has proposed an investment project characterized by the following estimates of revenues and costs in thousands of dollars:

Year	Revenues	Costs
0	—	$1,000
1	$ 600	$ 500
2	$1,200	—

The costs are incurred in the early years, while the revenues are generated in the later years. Assuming an interest rate of 8 percent, the net present value of the project is easily calculated (costs are entered as negative cash flow):

$$\text{NPV} = -1,000 + \frac{100}{1 + .08} + \frac{1,200}{(1 + .08)^2}$$
$$= -1,000 + 93 + 1,029$$
$$= \$122,000$$

Hence, NPV is positive and increases the value of the business.

2. The definitional equation for calculating internal rate of return (IRR) is:

$$\sum_{t=0}^{T} \frac{R_t - C_t}{(1 + r)^t} = 0,$$

where r = internal rate of return (IRR),
 R_t = revenues received in year t,
 C_t = costs paid for in year t, and
 T = length of the planning horizon.

To illustrate the IRR, we shall return to the example used for NPV.

To calculate the IRR for that particular investment project, we must solve the following equation for r:

$$-1,000 + \frac{100}{1 + r} + \frac{1,200}{(1 + r)^2} = 0.$$

The answer, which can be found easily by trial and error, is approximately 14.6 percent. Hence, if the market rate of interest were 14.6 percent, NPV would be equal to zero and the company would be indifferent about investing in this project.

3. See chapter 10 of Thomas H. Naylor, John M. Vernon, and Kenneth L. Wertz, *Managerial Economics: Corporate Economics and Strategy* (New York: McGraw-Hill, 1983).

4. This section draws heavily on discussions with William W. Reynolds, economics consultant of Shell Oil Company, and on two lectures he gave to the New York and Chicago chapters of the Planning Executives Institute in the fall of 1983.

5. Based in part on a lecture given by Abraham Katz, director of Planning Systems for IBM, at a seminar sponsored by the Planning Executives Institute in New York City, September 29, 1983.

6. Martin J. Gerra, Jr., "Integrating the International Environment into Corporate Strategy," in *Portfolio Planning and Corporate Strategy*, Thomas H. Naylor and Michele H. Mann, eds. (Oxford, OH: Planning Executives Institute, 1983), p. 147.

7. Most of the information in this section was provided by Richard A.

Notes

Druckman, vice-president of Strategic Planning and Management Information Systems of the Squibb Pharmaceutical Products Group.

Chapter 5

1. Michael E. Porter, *Competitive Strategy* (New York: Free Press, 1980), p. 35.
2. Ibid., p. 35.
3. Ibid., pp. 37–38.
4. Ibid., p. 38.
5. Ibid., p. 267.
6. Ibid., p. 4.

Chapter 6

1. Michael E. Porter, *Competitive Strategy* (New York: Free Press, 1980), pp. 275–98.
2. We benefited from information and comments provided by Robert S. Springmier, former director of Corporate Planning and now controller of Dow-Corning Corporation, and from his article, "Planning as a Vehicle for Strategic Redirection in a Matrix Structure," *Implementation of Strategic Planning*, Peter Lorange, ed. (Englewood Cliffs, NJ: Prentice-Hall, 1982), pp. 194–205.
3. Based in part on an unpublished paper by William H. Hoffmann, manager, Organization Planning, of Alcoa. The paper was titled, "Matrix Organization in Alcoa," November 9, 1981.
4. Based on the "1983 Annual Report of the Dow Chemical Company" and on an unpublished paper entitled, "The Matrix Organization as One Company Does It," by Roger Gohrband, director, Corporate Planning and Business Development, Dow Chemical Company, November 9, 1981. The paper was presented at a meeting of the Conference Board in New York City on that date.
5. Based on two unpublished papers: John C. Marous, Jr., president, the Westinghouse Industries and International Group, "Matrix Management in the Global Marketplace," May 6, 1980; and Alan J. Melinger, director, International Marketing and Strategic Resources, Westinghouse Electric Corporation, "Exporting the Matrix Operation."
6. John C. Marous, Jr., "Matrix Management in the Global Marketplace," address to the 1980 Westinghouse management council. The Homestead, Hot Springs, VA, May 6, 1980, p. 2.

Notes

Chapter 7

1. Andrew S. Grove, *High Output Management* (New York: Random House, 1983).

2. Stanley M. Davis and Paul R. Lawrence, *Matrix* (Reading, MA: Addison-Wesley, 1977), pp. 56–57.

3. Cary Reich, "The Innovators," *The New York Times Magazine*, April 21, 1985, p. 75.

4. Ibid, p. 29.

5. Rollo May, *Freedom and Destiny* (New York: Dell Publications, 1981), p. 186.

6. Sara Riner, "The Airline That Shook the Industry," *The New York Times Magazine*, May 23, 1984, p. 27.

7. John Holusha "A Race for Greater Auto Profits," *New York Times*, September 30, 1984, section 3, p. 1.

8. Based on the description of Citibank's experience with matrix management, which appeared in Stanley M. Davis and Paul R. Lawrence's book, *Matrix* (see footnote 2, pp. 166–68, 207–22).

INDEX

Index

Index

Hewlett-Packard, 29, 60–61, 276n12
High Output Management (Grove), 239
High-technology firms, 44
Hoffman, William H., 216, 218–19, 279n3
Holusha, John, 280n6
Honeywell, 99
Hong Kong, Dow Chemical in, 221
Human resources: deployment of, 259; planning of, 257
Hungary, 57; economic reform in, 273

IBM, x, 3, 15, 40, 41, 99, 267–70, 276n1, 267n12, 278n5; career paths at, 261; competitive forces and, 31; computer simulation models used by, 82; corporate culture of, 239; entrepreneurial approach of, 29; foreign competition with, 55; government regulation and, 30–31, 56; international operations of, 57, 203, 205–8, 236, 238; matrix management of, 35, 36, 43; nonfinancial strategies of, 91; resource allocation of, 70, 142, 156–65, 171; staffing of, 259, 260; team building at, 251; technological change and, 56; zero-sum management of, 23
IFPS, 82
Implementation: of business strategy, 188–92; corporate culture and, 246–48; in divisional organization, 8; functional, 35; in functional organization, 5; gap between planning and, 38; international, 76–77; portfolio analysis and, 63–65; of portfolio strategies, 113, 116; at SCANA Corporation, 129; staffing and, 259; of strategic plans, 83–85; in strategy matrix, 10–12, 14

In Search of Excellence (Peters and Waterman), 35–36
Incentive pay, 263
Independent business units, 164–65
Indiana Standard, 154
Industry maturity, 106, 107
Inflation, 53, 54
Inflexibility, 30–32, 268, 274
Information, responsibility for flow of, 84
Information systems, 45–46, 50
Intel, x, 267, 268, 276n1, 276n12; corporate culture of, 239–41; matrix management of, 36, 43, 45; team building at, 251, 256; technological change and, 56
Interdependence: of businesses, *see* Business interdependence; functional, 71–73, 120, 129
Interest rates, 53
Internal rate of return (IRR), 138, 139, 141, 171, 278n2
International environment, 56–58
International management, 74–77, 202–38, 268; business dimension of, 217–18; case examples of, 208–36; functional dimension of, 221–22; geographic dimension of, 216–17, 221; organization development and, 257; product dimension of, 222–23; tools of, 223–25
Intrapreneurialism, 29
ITT, 89, 135

Japan: competition with, 17, 20, 157; IBM in, 165, 207; management practices in, 22, 274
Johnson, Lyndon Baines, 30
Justice Department, U.S., 30, 31, 56, 158, 269

Katz, Abraham, 158–59, 163, 278n5
Kawasaki, 22

285

Index

Nuclear Regulatory Commission, 26, 121, 130, 134
NWT Resources, 262

Objectives, 59–61; business strategy and, 74, 174–76; of diversification, 219–21; of Federal Express, 196; formulation of, 13, 78–80; of IBM, 162; implementation of, 83; of international management, 218; portfolio analysis and, 112, 113; resource allocation and, 69, 144; of SCANA Corporation, 123, 124; of Velsicol Chemical, 186–87, 191
Off-site planning meetings, 77–80; of Florida Power, 198; of SCANA Corporation, 122; of Velsicol Chemical, 184–85
OPEC, 56, 67
Opel, John R., 165
Operating units, 163
Oreffice, Paul F., 225–26
Organization development, 257–64; career paths and, 260–62; compensation and, 262–64; planning and, 258; staffing and, 258–60
Organization structure, 46–50; of SCANA Corporation, 122; of Velsicol Chemical, 178, 179; see also Divisional organization; Functional organization

Pan American World Airways, 206
Parry, Charles W., 215
Participatory management, 28, 33–35, 37, 275; business strategy and, 73, 199; corporate culture and, 241, 249; government regulations and, 55; in portfolio analysis, 115–16, 133–34; resource allocation and, 156, 172; of SCANA Corporation, 121, 130; of Squibb,

168–70; women in, 254; see also Matrix management
Penn Central Railroad, 53
Penn Square Bank, 54
People Express Airlines, 253, 256
Peters, Thomas J., 35–37, 276n8
Petroleum industry, 67; acquisitions in, 88; resource allocation in, 146–48; see also Shell Oil
Pharmaceutical industry: nonfinancial strategies of, 91; see also Squibb Pharmaceutical Group
Philosophy of management, 241–44, 270
Planning: corporate culture and, 241, 244; critiques of, 38; in divisional organization, 8; in functional organization, 5, 7; human resource, 257; international, 76–77, 210; multidimensional, 35, 37–39; operational, 128, 144; organization development and, 258; portfolio approach to, 16–17, 20–21; strategic, see Strategic planning; in strategy matrix, 10–14; zero-sum management and, 23
Planning Executive Institute, 278n4, 278n5
Porter, Michael E., 180, 181, 185–86, 205, 206, 279n1
Portfolio analysis, 62–66, 86–134, 268; acquisitions and divestitures in, 88–89; alternative approaches to, 92–94; case example of, 116–30; financial strategies and, 89–90; in international management, 206; nonfinancial strategies and, 90–92; strategies based on, 87–92; strategy matrix, 111–34
Portfolio models, 81, 82, 92, 94–111, 131–34, 148, 158, 168; benefits of, 108; experience curve in, 100–102; financial strategies and, 102–4; growth-share matrix in, 95–100; limitations of, 109–11, 171; resource allocation and, 137
Portfolio planning, 16–17, 20–21
Power balancing, 83–84
Pricing strategy, 197

287

Index